DEFENSE, SECURITY AND STRATEGIES

AIR CARGO SECURITY

DEFENSE, SECURITY AND STRATEGIES

Additional books in this series can be found on Nova's website under the Series tab.

Additional E-books in this series can be found on Nova's website under the E-books tab.

TRANSPORTATION ISSUES, POLICIES AND R&D

Additional books in this series can be found on Nova's website under the Series tab.

Additional E-books in this series can be found on Nova's website under the E-books tab.

DEFENSE, SECURITY AND STRATEGIES

AIR CARGO SECURITY

PIERRE TURRIÓN
EDITOR

Nova Science Publishers, Inc.
New York

Copyright © 2012 by Nova Science Publishers, Inc.

All rights reserved. No part of this book may be reproduced, stored in a retrieval system or transmitted in any form or by any means: electronic, electrostatic, magnetic, tape, mechanical photocopying, recording or otherwise without the written permission of the Publisher.

For permission to use material from this book please contact us:
Telephone 631-231-7269; Fax 631-231-8175
Web Site: http://www.novapublishers.com

NOTICE TO THE READER

The Publisher has taken reasonable care in the preparation of this book, but makes no expressed or implied warranty of any kind and assumes no responsibility for any errors or omissions. No liability is assumed for incidental or consequential damages in connection with or arising out of information contained in this book. The Publisher shall not be liable for any special, consequential, or exemplary damages resulting, in whole or in part, from the readers' use of, or reliance upon, this material. Any parts of this book based on government reports are so indicated and copyright is claimed for those parts to the extent applicable to compilations of such works.

Independent verification should be sought for any data, advice or recommendations contained in this book. In addition, no responsibility is assumed by the publisher for any injury and/or damage to persons or property arising from any methods, products, instructions, ideas or otherwise contained in this publication.

This publication is designed to provide accurate and authoritative information with regard to the subject matter covered herein. It is sold with the clear understanding that the Publisher is not engaged in rendering legal or any other professional services. If legal or any other expert assistance is required, the services of a competent person should be sought. FROM A DECLARATION OF PARTICIPANTS JOINTLY ADOPTED BY A COMMITTEE OF THE AMERICAN BAR ASSOCIATION AND A COMMITTEE OF PUBLISHERS.

Additional color graphics may be available in the e-book version of this book.

Library of Congress Cataloging-in-Publication Data

Air cargo security / editor, Pierre Turrión.
   p. cm.
   Includes index.
   ISBN 978-1-62100-054-9 (hardcover)
   1. Aeronautics, Commercial--United States--Freight. 2. Aeronautics--Security measures--Government policy--United States. I. Turrión, Pierre.
   HE9788.5.U5A596 2011
   387.7'44--dc23
                                                                 2011029314

Published by Nova Science Publishers, Inc. † New York

CONTENTS

Preface		vii
Chapter 1	Aviation Security: Background and Policy Options for Screening and Securing Air Cargo *Bart Elias*	1
Chapter 2	Screening and Securing Air Cargo: Background and Issues for Congress *Bart Elias*	55
Chapter 3	TSA Has Made Progress but Faces Challenges in Meeting the Statutory Mandate for Screening Air Cargo on Passenger Aircraft *United States Government Accountability Office*	81
Chapter 4	Testimony before the Subcommittee on Transportation Security, Committee on Homeland Security, House of Representatives Aviation Security: Progress Made, But Challenges Persist in Meeting the Screening Mandate for Air Cargo *United States Government Accountability Office*	137

Chapter 5	Statement of John Sammon Assistant Administrator for Transportation Sector Network Management Transportation Security Administration U.S. Department of Homeland Security Before the United ztates House of Representatives Committee on Homeland Security Subcommittee on Transportation Security	**151**
Index		**157**

PREFACE

This book examines aviation security with a focus on the background and policy options for screening and securing air cargo.

Chapter 1- The air cargo system is a complex, multi-faceted network that handles a vast amount of freight, express packages, and mail carried aboard passenger and all-cargo aircraft. The air cargo system is vulnerable to several security risks, including potential plots to place explosives aboard aircraft; illegal shipments of hazardous materials; criminal activities such as smuggling and theft; and potential hijackings and sabotage by persons with access to aircraft. Several procedural and technology-based initiatives to enhance air cargo security and deter terrorist and criminal threats have been put in place or are under consideration. Procedural initiatives include industry-wide consolidation of the "known shipper program"; increased cargo inspections; increased physical security of air cargo facilities; increased oversight of air cargo operations; security training for cargo workers; stricter controls over access to cargo aircraft and air cargo operations areas; improved tracking of cargo shipments along the entire supply chain; and expanded use of explosives detection canine teams for inspecting air cargo shipments. Technology being considered to improve air cargo security includes tamper-resistant and tamper-evident packaging and containers; explosive detection technologies adapted for use in the air cargo environment; blast-resistant cargo containers and aircraft hardening; and biometric systems for worker identification and access control.

Chapter 2- The October 2010 discovery of two explosive devices being prepared for loading on U.S.-bound all-cargo aircraft overseas has heightened concerns over the potential use of air cargo shipments to bomb passenger and all-cargo aircraft. The incidents have renewed policy debate over air cargo security measures and have prompted some policymakers to call for comprehensive screening of all air cargo, including shipments that travel on all-cargo aircraft.

Chapter 3- Billions of pounds of cargo are transported on U.S. passenger flights annually. The Department of Homeland Security's (DHS) Transportation Security Administration (TSA) is the primary federal agency responsible for securing the air cargo system. The 9/11 Commission Act of 2007 mandated DHS to establish a system to screen 100 percent of cargo flown on passenger aircraft by August 2010. As requested, GAO reviewed TSA's progress in meeting the act's screening mandate, and any related challenges it faces for both domestic (cargo transported within and from the United States) and inbound cargo (cargo bound for the United States). GAO reviewed TSA's policies and procedures, interviewed TSA officials and air cargo industry stakeholders, and conducted site visits at five U.S. airports, selected based on size, among other factors.

Chapter 4- The Department of Homeland Security's (DHS) Transportation Security Administration (TSA) is the federal agency with primary responsibility for securing the air cargo system. The Implementing Recommendations of the 9/11 Commission Act of 2007 mandated DHS to establish a system to screen 100 percent of cargo flown on passenger aircraft by August 2010. GAO reviewed TSA's progress in meeting the act's screening mandate, and any related challenges it faces for both domestic (cargo transported within and from the United States) and inbound cargo (cargo bound for the United States). This statement is based on prior reports and testimonies issued from April 2007 through December 2010 addressing the security of the air cargo transportation system and selected updates made in February and March 2011. For the updates, GAO obtained information on TSA's air cargo security programs and interviewed TSA officials.

Chapter 5- This is an edited, reformatted and augmented version of Statement given by John Sammon, Assistant Administrator for Transportation Sector Network Management, before the United States House of Representatives Committee on Homeland Security Subcommittee on Transportation Security, dated March 9, 2011.

In: Air Cargo Security
Editor: Pierre Turrión

ISBN: 978-1-62100-054-9
© 2012 Nova Science Publishers, Inc.

Chapter 1

AVIATION SECURITY: BACKGROUND AND POLICY OPTIONS FOR SCREENING AND SECURING AIR CARGO[*]

Bart Elias

SUMMARY

The air cargo system is a complex, multi-faceted network that handles a vast amount of freight, express packages, and mail carried aboard passenger and all-cargo aircraft. The air cargo system is vulnerable to several security risks, including potential plots to place explosives aboard aircraft; illegal shipments of hazardous materials; criminal activities such as smuggling and theft; and potential hijackings and sabotage by persons with access to aircraft. Several procedural and technology-based initiatives to enhance air cargo security and deter terrorist and criminal threats have been put in place or are under consideration. Procedural initiatives include industry-wide consolidation of the "known shipper program"; increased cargo inspections; increased physical security of air cargo facilities; increased oversight of air cargo operations; security training for cargo workers; stricter controls over access to cargo aircraft and air cargo operations areas; improved tracking of cargo shipments along the entire supply chain; and expanded use of

---

[*] This is an edited, reformatted and augmented version of a Congressional Research Service publication RL34390, dated February 25, 2008.

explosives detection canine teams for inspecting air cargo shipments. Technology being considered to improve air cargo security includes tamper-resistant and tamper-evident packaging and containers; explosive detection technologies adapted for use in the air cargo environment; blast-resistant cargo containers and aircraft hardening; and biometric systems for worker identification and access control.

The Aviation and Transportation Security Act (ATSA, P.L. 107-71) contains general provisions for cargo screening, inspection, and security measures. Cargo carried in passenger airplanes must be screened or its security otherwise ensured. In practice, the Transportation Security Administration (TSA) has relied heavily on known shipper protocols to prevent shipments of cargo from unknown sources on passenger aircraft. ATSA also mandated development of a security plan for all-cargo operations. The TSA's air cargo security plan has focused on risk-based methods for assessing cargo shipments and targeting physical inspections. The National Intelligence Reform Act of 2004 (P.L. 108-458) included provisions establishing a pilot program for evaluating the deployment of blast-resistant cargo containers; promoting the research, development, and deployment of enhanced air cargo security technology; evaluating international air cargo threats; and finalizing operational regulations of air cargo security. Those regulations, finalized by the TSA in 2006, require use of an industry-wide known shipper database, background checks of air cargo workers, and enhanced security measures at air cargo operations areas. In addition to these measures, Congress has provided appropriations to hire more canine teams and cargo inspectors to step up cargo screening and regulatory inspections.

Appropriations legislation over the past four years has called for continued increases to the amounts of air cargo placed on passenger airplanes that is physically screened. The Implementing Recommendations of the 9/11 Commission Act of 2007 (P.L. 110-53) requires the DHS to establish a system to physically screen 100% of all air cargo within three years, with an interim requirement of screening 50% of air cargo within 18 months of enactment. The act also directs the TSA to implement a program for deploying blast-resistant cargo containers for use by air carriers on a risk-managed basis.

OVERVIEW OF THE AIR CARGO SYSTEM

The air cargo system is a complex, multi-faceted network responsible for moving a vast amount of freight, express packages, and mail carried aboard passenger and all-cargo aircraft. The air cargo system consists of a large, complex distribution network linking manufacturers and shippers to freight forwarders and then on to airport sorting and cargo handling facilities where shipments are loaded and unloaded from aircraft. Business and consumer demand for the fast and efficient shipment of goods has fueled rapid growth in the air cargo industry over the past 25 years.

In FY2006, about 10.5 million tons of freight cargo were shipped by air within the United States, and another 8.5 million tons were shipped on international flights to and from the United States on both passenger and all-cargo aircraft.[1] In addition to this, over half a million tons of mail was carried on aircraft, roughly 460,000 tons on domestic flights and 140,000 tons on international flights to and from the United States. The combined weight of freight and mail enplaned on domestic and international flights from 2003 through 2006 is shown in *Figure 1*.

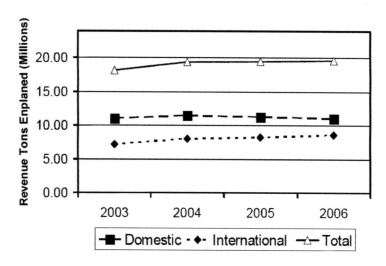

Figure 1. Freight and Mail Enplaned on Domestic and International Flights (2003-2006).

Since 1980, the growth in freight mileage for air cargo, measured in terms of ton-miles transported on an annual basis, has far outpaced growth in any other transportation mode.[2] While domestic growth in the volume of air cargo shipments has been relatively, and somewhat unexpectedly, flat over the past few years, it is estimated that domestic air cargo shipments, expressed in terms of revenue ton miles (RTMs), will continue their historic growth trends and increase another 58% by FY2020 compared to FY2006 levels. Internationally, cargo shipments have seen steady growth over the past few years and are anticipated to increase 135% by FY2020 compared to FY2006 levels. The volume of air cargo shipments since FY1999 and the forecast volume of air cargo through 2020 is shown in *Figure 2*.

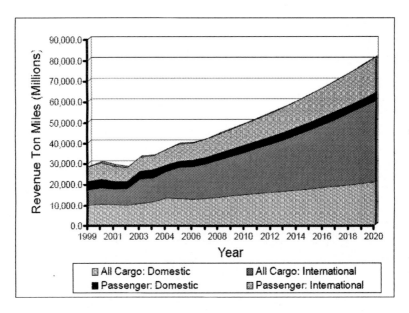

Figure 2. Air Cargo Shipments: Historic Data and Forecasts (FY1999-FY2020).

In 2005, air cargo comprised about 0.4% by weight of all freight movement in the United States.[3] While this percentage may seem small, it is much greater than the 0.07% percent of freight that traveled by air in 1965, indicating that not only is the volume of air cargo increasing significantly, but so is the percent of total freight movements that travel by air. Since 1980, the freight mileage of goods shipped by air has increased by 240%.[4] Air cargo shipments also make up a significant percent of the total value of cargo shipments. In 2002, while air freight movements accounted for only about 0.3% of total domestic freight shipments by weight, these shipments accounted for 4.3% of the total value of freight shipped within the United States.[5] In terms of global trade, air cargo accounted for 25.3% of the value of goods shipped to and from the United States, surpassed only by maritime shipping, which accounted for 43.5% of the import/export value of cargo in 2005.[6] However, by weight, nearly 78% of imports and exports travel by water, compared to just 0.4% by air. These statistics reflect the fact that international air cargo plays a major role in the transport of high-value, time-sensitive, light-weight imports and exports. Such items include consumer electronics, electronic components for industry and manufacturing, flowers, and other high-value perishable foods and goods, to name a few examples. The speed of delivery afforded by air cargo support just-in-time demand for such goods in a global marketplace, allowing far-away manufacturing and distribution sites to rapidly deliver items to businesses and end customers worldwide. These unique characteristic of the air cargo industry are important considerations for policymakers in addressing air cargo security needs without unduly impeding the flow of commerce that travels by air, particularly as the size and complexity of the air cargo system continues to expand.

SECURITY SCREENING AND INSPECTIONS OF AIR CARGO: POLICY DEBATE AND OPERATIONAL CHALLENGES

Given the sheer volume of cargo that must be expediently processed and loaded on aircraft, it has been generally argued that physical screening of all air cargo using explosives detection technologies, as is now required of checked passenger baggage, is likely to present significant logistic and operational challenges. In 2002, it was reported that TSA computer models estimated that, if full physical screening of cargo were implemented, only 4% of the daily volume of freight at airports could be processed due to the time that would be required to break down shipments, inspect them, and reassemble them for transport.[7] Since that time, considerable progress has been made to increase the amount of cargo placed on passenger airliners that is subject to physical screening and inspection. Also, the DHS has invested in several research and development initiatives to adapt explosives screening technologies for use in the air cargo environment. The results of these efforts are best described as a slow evolution of increasing inspections and screening of air cargo shipments placed on passenger aircraft since 2002, coupled with some promising opportunities to further increase cargo inspections and screening through an array of various techniques and technologies. This is in contrast to baggage screening, which relies predominantly on a single technology, Explosives Detection System (EDS), as was required under the Aviation and Transportation Security Act (ATSA; P.L. 107-71).

Over the next few years, there is likely to be a more intense focus on developing and tailoring technologies and procedures for screening and inspecting air cargo to meet a mandate in the Implementing Recommendations of the 9/11 Commission Act of 2007 (P.L. 110-53) that requires 100% screening of all cargo placed on passenger aircraft by August 2010, with an interim requirement of screening 50% of such cargo by February 2009. Unlike baggage screening operations which are, for the most part, conducted by TSA personnel, cargo inspections and screening operations are conducted largely by employees of the airlines and freight shippers, with the TSA responsible for oversight of these functions. In 2004, the National Intelligence Reform Act of 2004 (P.L. 108-458) required the TSA to pursue screening technologies and enhance security procedures to improve the inspection, screening, and tracking of air cargo on passenger aircraft as recommended by the 9/11 Commission. Since then, implementing increased oversight and inspections of air cargo operations coupled with more stringent regulations for air cargo carriers and freight forwarders has been a priority for the TSA.

Congressional appropriators have provided increased funding for inspections, screening, and tracking of air cargo, and for research, development, and pilot testing of various explosives screening techniques and technologies to increase the amount of air cargo that undergoes physical inspection. While the TSA does not divulge the percentage of cargo that undergoes physical inspection, language in the FY2005 Homeland Security Appropriations Act (P.L. 108-334) called for at least tripling the amount of cargo placed on passenger aircraft that was inspected at that time. FY2006 appropriations language (P.L. 109-90) directed the TSA to take all possible measures — including the certification, procurement, and deployment of screening systems — to inspect and screen air cargo on passenger aircraft and increase the percentage of cargo inspected beyond the level mandated in the FY2005 appropriations measure.

FY2007 appropriations language (P.L. 109-295) directs the TSA to work with industry stakeholders to develop standards and protocols to increase the use of explosives detection equipment for screening air cargo. The FY2008 Omnibus Appropriations Act (P.L. 110-161) directed the DHS to research, develop and procure new technologies to screen and inspect air cargo loaded on passenger aircraft, and utilize existing checked baggage explosives detection equipment and screeners to the greatest extent practicable to screen air cargo until dedicated air cargo screening technologies can be developed and deployed. The act requires the DHS to work with air carriers and airports to ensure that the screening of cargo carried on passenger aircraft continually increases, and requires the DHS to submit quarterly reports detailing the incremental progress being made toward achieving the mandated 100% screening of cargo placed on passenger aircraft.

The mandate for 100% screening contained in P.L. 110-53 requires inspection of all air cargo placed on passenger aircraft in a manner that provides a level of security equivalent to the screening of passenger checked baggage. The legislative language specifically defines screening in this context to mean a physical examination or other non-intrusive methods of assessing whether cargo poses a threat to transportation security. The act identifies specific methods of screening that would be acceptable in meeting this requirement, including the use of x-ray systems, explosives detection systems, explosives trace detection, TSA-certified explosives detection canine teams, and physical searches conducted in conjunction with manifest verifications. Additional methods may be approved by the TSA. However, the provision specifically prohibits the use of cargo documents and known shipper verification by themselves as being acceptable screening methods. In other words, the provision clarifies that the screening of cargo is to involve some sort of inspection process that cannot be met solely by a records verification of shipment contents or shipper status. The language does, however, leave open the possibility that the TSA could implement some other non-intrusive methods for assessing whether cargo poses a risk that would not necessarily involve the use of physical screening technologies. It is, at this point, unclear what specific approach the TSA will take to meet this mandate. The TSA is required to promulgate regulations to meet these requirements and must provide justification for any exemptions to these air cargo screening requirements it may grant. Also, the GAO would be required to assess the methods used by the TSA in granting, modifying, or eliminating any exemptions to these requirements. The measure was generally opposed by various stakeholders in the air cargo industry who believe that its requirements are overly burdensome and costly.[8]

POLICY CONSIDERATIONS FOR SECURING ALL-CARGO OPERATIONS

While the primary policy focus of legislation to date has been on cargo carried aboard passenger aircraft, air cargo security also presents a challenge for all-cargo operators, there is some concern that heightened security measures for passenger aircraft may make all cargo aircraft a more attractive target to terrorists. However, unlike passenger operations where the threat from explosives introduced in air cargo represents the greatest perceived risk, the greatest perceived risk associated with air cargo operations is the potential for an individual or individuals with access to aircraft to hijack a large transport category aircraft to carry out a suicide attack against a ground target. Looking beyond aviation security, there is also a broader risk that terrorists may attempt to ship weapons, including possible weapons of mass destruction, into and within the United States using the global cargo distribution network. For example, various law enforcement and counterterrorism operations have shown how illegal sales and shipments of various weapons, such as shoulderfired missiles, may be facilitated by falsified shipping documents allowing such items to potentially wind up in international and domestic air cargo shipments. Homeland security policies and strategies may need to further consider the potential risks that air cargo operations, as well as passenger airlines cargo operations, may be exploited to facilitate the movement of terrorist weapons.

The largest all-cargo operators in the United States include FedEx, UPS, Atlas Air, Polar Air Cargo, Kallita Air, ABX Air, Evergreen International Airlines, Gemini Air Cargo, and World Airways.[9] In addition, some airlines with passenger service, such as Northwest Airlines and United, also have fleets of all-cargo aircraft. *Figure 3* shows the distribution of air freight shipments among passenger and all-cargo aircraft. Domestic operations make up about 57% of the total system-wide air cargo operations in the United States.

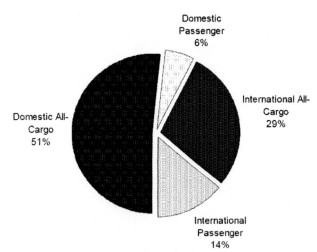

Source: CRS analysis of Bureau of Transportation Statistics, Air Carrier Statistics, T-100 Domestic and International Market Data (All Carriers).

Figure 3. Distribution of Enplaned Freight Cargo on Passenger and All-Cargo Aircraft on Domestic and International Flights (2003-2006).

However, in recent years, only about 10% of domestic air freight has been carried aboard passenger aircraft within the United States. Ninety percent is carried aboard all cargo aircraft. In international operations, passenger aircraft have played a bigger role, carrying roughly one third of air freight shipments to and from the United States. The rest is carried aboard all cargo aircraft which account for 67% of the international air freight volume.

While passenger airlines continue to play an important role in carrying air freight, the percentage of air cargo carried on passenger aircraft has continued to drop since September 11, 2001. Industry analysts expect that there will likely be a further decline in the proportion of freight carried on passenger aircraft as a result of new federal requirements to achieve 100% screening of all cargo placed on passenger aircraft by August 2010. This may have a greater impact on international air cargo operations which rely more heavily on the use of passenger aircraft. Experts note, however, that if effective security measures are not implemented and a passenger aircraft bomb introduced in air cargo were to take down an airplane, lawmakers and regulators may respond by imposing significant restrictions on passenger aircraft air cargo, possibly banning cargo on passenger aircraft altogether.[10] Regardless of whether passenger air cargo is specifically targeted or not, the long term outlook points to a continued shift toward increased reliance on all-cargo aircraft, both domestically and in international operations.

Since September 11, 2001, a variety of air cargo security measures have been put in place or are under consideration. The primary purpose of these security measures is to mitigate: (1) the potential risks associated with the contents of cargo placed on passenger as well as all-cargo aircraft; and (2) the risks associated with individuals given a high level of access to aircraft to carry out cargo operations. This report will examine the key security risks associated with air cargo operations and options for mitigating these risks.

AIR CARGO SECURITY RISKS

Potential risks associated with air cargo shipments and operations include the possible introduction of explosives and incendiary devices in cargo placed aboard aircraft; shipment of undeclared or undetected hazardous materials aboard aircraft; cargo crime including theft and smuggling; and aircraft hijackings and sabotage by individuals with access to aircraft. As previously noted, the security risk associated with air cargo is believed to be considerably different for passenger airline operations, where the greatest perceived threat is the introduction of an explosive device through an air cargo shipment, and all cargo operations, where the greatest perceived threat is the potential hijacking of a large all cargo aircraft to carry out a suicide attack against a ground target.

Explosives and Incendiary Devices. Undetected explosive or incendiary devices placed in air cargo are potential threats to aircraft, particularly passenger aircraft that carry cargo consignments. Experts have warned that air cargo may be a potential target for terrorists because screening and inspection of air cargo is currently not as extensive as required screening of passengers and checked baggage.

For this reason, Congress has pushed the TSA to increase screening and inspections of air cargo, and recently mandated 100% screening of all cargo placed on passenger aircraft by August 2010 (see P.L. 110-53).

Cargo carried aboard passenger aircraft may be at particular risk since passenger aircraft are generally regarded as highly attractive targets to terrorists and have been attacked in the past. However, some aviation security and counterterrorism experts regard placing explosives in air cargo as a less appealing option to terrorists because typically a specific flight cannot be targeted without the assistance of an individual with access to aircraft. Furthermore, experts generally believe that all-cargo aircraft are less appealing targets to terrorists because an attack against an all-cargo aircraft is not likely to result in mass casualties and generate the degree of public and media attention that a bombing of a commercial passenger aircraft would have.

Aircraft bombings remain a considerable concern, although recent aircraft bombings attempts and plots have not specifically involved the introduction of a bomb placed in air cargo. Rather, at present the specific aviation security focus has been in response to attempts to carry on or assemble improvised explosives devices in the passenger cabin. For example, the December 22, 2001, attempted shoe bombing aboard a American Airlines Boeing 767 on a trans-Atlantic Paris to Miami flight and the foiled plot to allegedly bomb U.S.-bound airliners from the United Kingdom in August 2006 has heightened concerns over possible terrorist bombings of passenger aircraft.

Historically, bombings of U.S. airliners have been rare and have mostly involved bombs placed in either the aircraft passenger cabin or in checked passenger baggage. The most catastrophic bombing of a U.S. airliner was the December 21, 1988 crash of Pan Am flight 103, a Boeing 747, over Lockerbie, Scotland that was attributed to an explosive device placed in a baggage container in the airplane's forward hold.[11] Investigation of the deadliest bombing of a passenger aircraft, the June 23, 1985 downing of Air India flight 182 off the coast of Ireland, similarly revealed evidence of an explosive device that was most likely introduced in checked baggage and placed in the aircraft's forward cargo hold.[12] While the historic risk has been tied to passenger baggage, and the current aviation security policy emphasis is on improvised explosives in the passenger cabin, efforts to protect against these threats may make cargo a more attractive option for terrorists. The most notable event involving detonation of an explosive device transported as cargo aboard an airliner in the United States was the November 15, 1979 explosion aboard an American Airlines Boeing 727 that made a successful emergency landing at Dulles Airport following the incident. This event, while tied to an individual terrorist but not a terrorist organization, did not intend to target the aircraft. Rather, investigation revealed that the device was contained in a parcel shipped by U.S. mail that the Federal Bureau of Investigation (FBI) linked to convicted "Unabomber," Theodore Kaczynski.[13]

While using cargo as a means to place explosive or incendiary devices aboard aircraft has historically been rare, heightened screening of passengers, baggage, and aircraft may make cargo a more attractive means for terrorists to place these devices aboard aircraft, including all-cargo aircraft as well as passenger aircraft, in the future.

Investigations have suggested that al Qaeda terrorists had an interest in bombing allcargo aircraft prior to September 11, 2001, and were planning to bomb U.S.-bound cargo flights in an operation run out of the Philippines.[14] Given al Qaeda's continued interest in bombing aircraft and indications that they have already considered placing bombs in cargo, the specific vulnerability of air cargo is an issue of particular concern.

However, as previously noted, some terrorism experts believe that placing explosives or incendiary devices in cargo may be less appealing because it would be difficult to target specific flights without the cooperation of individuals with access to aircraft such as cargo workers. Thus, increased efforts to perform background checks of workers with access to aircraft and increased physical security around air cargo operations may further mitigate the threat of explosives and incendiary devices.

In 2006, the TSA finalized rules requiring fingerprint-based criminal history records checks (CHRCs) and terrorist screening of individuals working in cargo operations areas, and workers at freight forwarding companies that handle the routing of air cargo. Additionally, the use of hardened cargo containers capable of withstanding internal bomb blasts are being evaluated and may also provide a means of mitigating the risks of explosives and incendiary devices. The 9/11 Commission specifically recommended the deployment of at least one hardened cargo container in each passenger aircraft to mitigate the potentially catastrophic consequences of a bomb carried in air cargo.[15] Under a provision in the National Intelligence Reform Act of 2004 (P.L. 108-458), a pilot program was established to evaluate this concept. A provision in the Implementing the 9/11 Commission Recommendations Act of 2007 (P.L. 110-53) directed the TSA to provide an evaluation of the pilot program and, based on its findings, implement a program to pay for, provide, and maintain blastresistant cargo containers for use by air carriers on a risk-managed basis.

Hazardous Materials[16]

Despite increased Federal Aviation Administration (FAA) and Department of Transportation (DOT) oversight and enforcement efforts, undeclared and undetected shipments of hazardous materials continue to pose a significant safety problem for air carriers. Most explosives and gases are prohibited aboard aircraft, however many properly handled hazardous materials are permitted aboard passenger and all-cargo aircraft within specified quantity limitations.[17]

Risks are introduced when hazardous materials are not declared leading to the potential transport of prohibited materials by air or improper handling of hazardous goods during loading and while in transit. The dangers of undetected and improperly handled hazardous materials in air cargo shipments were highlighted by the May 11, 1996 crash of a ValuJet DC-9 in the Florida Everglades. The National Transportation Safety Board (NTSB) determined that improperly carried oxygen generators ignited an intense fire in one of the airplane's cargo holds leading to the crash and issued several safety recommendations for improving the handling and tracking of hazardous materials to prevent improper carriage aboard passenger aircraft.[18]

While safety concerns regarding hazardous cargo shipments aboard passenger aircraft are of particular concern, preventing unauthorized shipments of hazardous materials is a challenge for all-cargo aircraft operators as well. About 75% of hazardous materials shipped by aircraft are carried aboard all-cargo aircraft, while the remaining 25% is shipped on passenger aircraft.[19] Enhanced air cargo security measures may also improve air cargo safety by increasing the detection of undeclared hazardous materials through screening and inspections of cargo shipments and related paperwork.

Cargo Crime

Cargo crimes include theft of goods transported as cargo, and shipment and smuggling of contraband, counterfeit, and pirated goods through the cargo distribution network. It has been estimated that direct losses due to cargo theft across all transportation modes total between $15 and $30 billion annually in the United States.[20] The large range in this estimate reflects the fact that cargo theft and other cargo crime has not historically been a specific designated crime category, and therefore reliable statistics on cargo theft are not available. A provision in the USA PATRIOT Improvement and Reauthorization Act (P.L. 109-177), however, required the Department of Justice to establish a separate category for cargo theft in the Uniform Crime Reporting System. The act also refines relevant statutes and increases criminal penalties for cargo theft and stowaways.

The large estimated level of cargo theft and other cargo crimes is indicative of potential weaknesses in cargo security, including air cargo security. Specific weaknesses in air cargo security have been highlighted in several high profile investigations of cargo theft. For example, major cargo and baggage theft rings have been uncovered at JFK International Airport in New York, Logan International Airport in Boston, and at Miami International Airport.[21] In addition to theft, smuggling has also been a problem for air cargo security. Smuggling of contraband, counterfeit, and pirated goods undermines legal markets and reduces government tax and tariff revenues. Smuggling operations are often linked to organized crime, and may provide support for terrorist activities.[22] A large portion of cargo crime is either committed by or with the assistance of cargo workers. Therefore, increased security measures such as conducting more stringent or more frequent background checks of cargo workers and enhancing physical security of cargo operations areas are likely to reduce cargo crimes and improve the capability to detect criminal activity in air cargo operations. A review of transportation security needs for combating cargo crime identified six key issues regarding cargo security:

- a lack of effective cargo theft reporting systems;
- weaknesses in current transportation crime laws and prosecution;
- a lack of understanding regarding the nature of cargo crime by governments and industry;
- inadequate support for cargo theft task forces;
- a need to improve local law enforcement expertise on cargo theft;and

- the need for more effective cargo security technology including cargo tracking systems, tamper-evident and tamper-resistant seals, high-speed screening devices, and integration of security technology into supply chain management systems.[23]

While some of these issues may be addressed through the Department of Justice's approach to meeting the mandate for uniformly reporting cargo crimes, concerns over the adequacy of law enforcement approaches to combating cargo crime and the implementation of cargo security technologies remain. Addressing these issues specific to cargo crime may also improve overall cargo security and could deter terrorist threats to cargo shipments. While these recommendations are directed toward cargo crime issues in all modes of transportation, they could also be particularly applicable to air cargo security where other security concerns such as explosive and incendiary device detection, hazardous materials detection, and deterring hijackings and sabotage may also be addressed through the implementation of tighter controls to deter cargo crime.

Aircraft Hijacking and Sabotage

Individuals with access to aircraft may pose a risk of potential hijackings and aircraft sabotage. Instances of hijackings by individuals with access to aircraft have been extremely rare, but include two examples of particularly violent incidents by disgruntled individuals who had access to aircraft that facilitated their plots. A particularly dramatic hijacking attempt by an individual with access to aircraft and cargo operations facilities occurred on April 7, 1994.[24] An off-duty Federal Express flight engineer attempted to hijack a FedEx DC-10 aircraft and crash it into the company's Memphis, Tennessee headquarters. The hijacker boarded the airplane in Memphis under the guise of seeking free transportation (a practice known in the industry as deadheading) to San Jose, California. His only luggage was a guitar case that concealed hammers, mallets, a knife, and a spear gun. At the time there was no requirement or company procedure to screen or inspect personnel with access to cargo aircraft or their baggage. The flight crew thwarted the hijacker's attempt to take over the airplane by force and made a successful emergency landing in Memphis despite serious injuries to all three flight crew members.

Individuals have also used their access to aircraft credentials to bypass existing security measures in airport terminals to carry out crimes, including aircraft hijackings and sabotage. In a particularly tragic example, on December 7, 1987, a PSA regional jet crashed near San Luis Obispo, California killing all 43 people on board.[25] Investigation revealed that a disgruntled former USAir employee, recently fired for alleged theft, used his employee identification, which had not been returned, to bypass airport security with a loaded handgun. At altitude, he shot his former supervisor who was a passenger on the airplane. He then entered the flight deck, shot the two pilots, and then shot himself after putting the airplane into a crash dive. At the time, airline employees were allowed to bypass airport security checkpoints. At many airports today, employees with unescorted access privileges to security identification display areas (SIDAs) may access secured areas and aircraft without being subject to physical screening. Specific screening procedures for airport workers vary from airport to airport and are part of the airport's TSA security program, which is considered security sensitive. Collecting airport access credentials from terminated employees remains a problem to this day. However, a provision in the FY2008 Omnibus Appropriations Act (P.L. 110-161) establishes civil penalties for airport contractors and vendors that fail to collect access credentials and notify the airport of employee terminations within 24 hours.

Since these incidents, airport and air cargo security regulations have been tightened to establish better controls over aircraft access including background checks and, in some cases, routine or random physical screening of individuals with access to aircraft. Background checks are required for workers with unescorted access to both passenger and air cargo aircraft. However, without full screening of air cargo and airport personnel, the potential still exists for persons with access to aircraft to pass weapons inside the secured areas of airports. Under recently imposed regulations, all-cargo operators must take steps to prevent unauthorized individuals from accessing aircraft and to ensure that crewmembers and individuals carried aboard large all-cargo aircraft are prevented or deterred from carrying weapons, explosives, or other destructive items on board aircraft.[26]

As mentioned earlier, heightened security measures on passenger aircraft since September 11, 2001 could make all-cargo aircraft more attractive to terrorists seeking to hijack large airplanes. Currently, federal air marshals are not deployed on allcargo aircraft, and cargo airplanes are not required to have hardened cockpit doors so long as alterative TSA-approved security measures are implemented to control access to aircraft and the flight deck while an airplane is on the ground. Vision 100 (P.L. 108-176) expanded the Federal Flight Deck Officer program to include pilots of all-cargo aircraft. This program trains and deputizes pilots to carry firearms to protect the flight deck against a terrorist attack.

Sabotage, such as tampering with, disabling, or destroying flight-critical systems and aircraft components, by individuals with access to aircraft is also a potential risk.

Although, this is not generally considered a significant threat because of the level of knowledge regarding aircraft systems needed to sabotage flight critical systems, the degree of redundancy of flight critical systems on modern transport category airplanes[27], and the existing capabilities to detect sabotage attempts through aircraft systems checks, pre-flight inspections, and maintenance checks. While numerous cases of sabotage by disgruntled employees have been documented, these incidents of aircraft tampering have typically been discovered during pre-flight inspections resulting in aircraft groundings and delays and costly repairs, but have not resulted in catastrophes. Such incidents have not been linked to terrorism.

CARGO SCREENING AND INSPECTION

Screening and inspection of air cargo may be an effective means for detecting explosives, incendiary devices, and hazardous materials in air cargo. The Aviation and Transportation Security Act (ATSA, P.L. 107-71) requires the screening of all property, including mail and cargo, carried aboard passenger aircraft in the United States. ATSA also specified that, as soon as practicable, a system must be implemented to screen, inspect, or otherwise ensure the security of all cargo transported in all-cargo aircraft. However, the GAO noted that the TSA lacked specific long-term goals and performance targets for cargo security.[28] In response, the TSA has developed an air cargo security strategic plan and has proposed comprehensive regulations designed to enhance air cargo security. The TSA's strategy centers on risk-based assessments and targeted physical screening of cargo based on risk as well as increased random inspections of shipments.

While ATSA established such a requirement, it is important to note that this has not been interpreted to require physical screening or inspection of cargo shipments carried aboard passenger aircraft. Rather, in implementing the security procedures for cargo carried aboard passenger airplanes, the TSA has relied extensively on the use of "known shipper" programs to prevent the shipment of cargo from unknown sources aboard passenger aircraft. Initially, air carriers and freight forwarders maintained their own lists of shippers that had established known and trustworthy business relationships to screen shipments placed on passenger aircraft. However, under rules finalized in 2006, airlines and freight forwarders must now use an industry-wide database of known shippers to clear shipments before they can be placed on passenger aircraft. However, some Members of Congress have expressed continued concern over applying targeted risk-based screening to cargo shipments placed on passenger aircraft. Through appropriations legislation, Congress has continually pressed the TSA to increase the percentage of cargo carried on passenger aircraft that is inspected, and has directed the DHS to invest in the research, development, and deployment of explosives screening technologies tailored for air cargo. As previously noted, the Implementing the 9/11 Commission Recommendations Act of 2007 (P.L. 110-53) establishes specific requirements and a timetable for implementing 100% physical screening or inspection of air cargo carried aboard passenger aircraft.

Current aviation security regulations require each passenger aircraft operator and indirect air carrier[29] to develop a security program for acceptance and screening of cargo to prevent or deter the carriage of unauthorized explosives or incendiaries.

However, the volume of air cargo handled and the distributed nature of the air cargo system presents significant challenges for screening and inspecting air cargo.

Presently, in the United States, about 50 air carriers transport air cargo on passenger aircraft handling cargo from nearly 2 million shippers per day.[30] About 80% of these shippers use freight forwarders who operate about 10,000 facilities across the country.[31] Since the air cargo industry has contended that 100% screening of all air cargo is not a practical solution with currently available technology, up until now security programs have relied primarily on pre-screening of cargo to identify shipments for targeted physical screening and inspection. The TSA has adopted a risk-based strategy that relies heavily on the known shipper process. The TSA had planned to include other factors in its cargo risk assessment through the use of a freight assessment system that it has been developing, based in part on CBP's targeting methods However, given the new mandate for achieving 100% physical screening of passenger air cargo, the future plans for the risk-based freight assessment system seem somewhat uncertain. Nonetheless, risk-based approaches remain a cornerstone of the TSA approach to air cargo security, and more broadly aviation security in general.

The TSA is currently working toward fully implementing its Air Cargo Strategic Plan, which was released in November 2003.[32] In keeping with the risk-based approach of implementing air cargo security measures typified in the known shipper concept, the core elements of this plan consist of: improving shipper and supply chain security through improved vetting of shippers and freight forwarders; enhancing cargo pre-screening processes; developing and deploying appropriate screening technologies to conduct targeted air cargo inspections; and implementing appropriate facility security measures. In addition to the known-shipper system, the TSA is also developing a more comprehensive targeting tool for air cargo, known as the "Freight Assessment System." While few details of this systems have been publicly disclosed, the TSA had indicated that it expected to fully deploy this system sometime in 2008, but as previously noted, the mandate for 100% screening of passenger air cargo may alter these plans.[33]

The Known Shipper Program

The principal means for pre-screening or profiling cargo has been through the use of air carrier and freight forwarder "known shipper" programs. In May 2006, the TSA issued a final rule establishing an industry-wide known shipper database for vetting all shipments placed on passenger aircraft.[34] Previously, some air carriers and indirect air carriers had voluntarily participated in a system using a central database of known shippers to vet cargo destined for passenger aircraft as required under ATSA. Other air carriers and freight forwarders relied on internal databases and security protocols approved by TSA for determining whether shipments bound for a passenger airplane come from known sources and that shippers have adequate security measures in place to protect the integrity of those shipments.

Known shipper programs were created to establish procedures for differentiating trusted shippers, known to a freight forwarder or air carrier through prior business dealings, from unknown shippers who have conducted limited or no prior business with a freight forwarder or air carrier. Using this system, packages from unknown shippers can then be identified for additional screening and inspection. Currently, shipments from unknown sources are prohibited from passenger aircraft.

Additionally, air carriers and freight forwarders must refuse to transport any cargo from shippers, including known shippers, that refuse to give consent for searching and inspecting the cargo. ATSA provides for use of known shipper programs as an alternate means for ensuring the security of cargo carried aboard passenger aircraft in lieu of screening of property by federal government employees prior to aircraft boarding.

The development of known shipper programs was prompted by industry experts and Congress in the mid-1990s who recognized that increased controls over air cargo shipments were needed to better ensure air cargo safety and security. Key concerns included the need for increased compliance with guidelines for the shipment of hazardous materials and the need to deter terrorists from using cargo as a means to place explosives or incendiary devices on aircraft. In addition, congressional hearings on the 1996 Valujet accident concluded that air cargo safety could only be achieved through a comprehensive inspection program encompassing all components of the air cargo network.[35]

In December 1996, the FAA's Aviation Security Advisory Committee (ASAC) Security Baseline Working Group issued a series of recommendations that formed the basis for FAA's effort to strengthen air cargo safety and security.

Recommendations issued by the working group regarding air cargo security included tightening the definition of a "known shipper"; using profiles to review the shipments of known shippers and apply additional security measures; and exploring technologies to develop a profile to be applied to cargo shipments. The White House Commission on Aviation Safety and Security, formed after the 1996 crash of TWA Flight 800 and commonly referred to as the Gore Commission, urged the adoption of the recommendations made by the FAA's Baseline Working Group regarding the profiling of "known" and "unknown"shippers.[36] As part of FAA's efforts in air cargo safety and security, a "known shipper" program was subsequently established, outlining procedures for freight forwarders and air carriers to review the security practices of known frequent customers and establish a cargo security plan for handling cargo from known and unknown shippers. With the passage of ATSA, oversight of cargo security measures was transferred from the FAA to the TSA. The TSA has continued to rely on known shipper programs as a principle means for prescreening air cargo.

A review of aviation security after the September 11, 2001 terrorist attacks by the DOT Office of the Inspector General, drew attention to the vulnerabilities of air cargo and questioned the overall effectiveness of the known shipper program.[37] In Congressional testimony following the terrorist attacks of September 11, 2001, DOT Inspector General, Kenneth Mead, referenced a 1998 report by the DOT Office of the Inspector General documenting a high rate of non-compliance with hazardous materials regulations and cargo security requirements across the air cargo industry and a lack of industry oversight to ensure that security procedures were carried out by cargo workers.[38] In 1998, the DOT Inspector General noted that FAA was making progress toward improving the policies, procedures, and controls over air cargo safety and security.[39] However, Mead testified that a follow-up audit revealed continued weaknesses in FAA's policy for allowing cargo on passenger aircraft. Several loopholes have been noted, including the relative ease of obtaining known shipper status, and the relative ease with which someone could pose as a known shipper by falsifying or counterfeiting shipping documents used to identify the source as a known shipper.[40]

Two central issues regarding the post-9/11 implementation of known shipper programs have been the adequacy of procedures for auditing and monitoring known shippers, and consideration of the potential need for a consolidated database of known shippers, as has now been created. Critics of known shipper programs have argued that relatively little investigation of known shippers is required to demonstrate that these shippers are trustworthy and have adequate security measures in place to ensure the integrity of their shipments.[41] Freight forwarders and air carriers have also questioned why extensive background checks and established relations with a particular customer are required to establish that the customer is a known shipper when that customer is already considered a known shipper to another air carrier or freight forwarder. Therefore, some had suggested a need for a standardized, centralized database of known shippers, as has now been created by the TSA. To address these concerns, the TSA initially instituted an industry-wide pilot program database of known shippers. This initiative poised the TSA to address congressional interest in establishing an industry-wide known shipper database that was included in language passed by the Senate during the 108th Congress (see S. 165, S. 2845 as passed by the Senate). The administration's subsequent initiatives in taking regulatory action to require an industry-wide known shipper database led Congress to ultimately drop the Senate-passed provision in the Intelligence Reform Act of 2004 (P.L. 108-458) that would have established a statutory requirement for establishing a standardized industry-wide known shipper program and database.

Congress instead settled on including language calling for the TSA to finalize its rulemaking on air cargo security, including the proposed establishment of the industry-wide known shipper database, by September 2005. Those rules were not finalized until May 2006, but are now being implemented, including the provision to establish an industry-wide known shipper database. The Congressional Budget Office (CBO) estimates that it will cost about $10 million per year to maintain the industry-wide database of known shippers.[42]

Physical Screening and Inspection

Another issue for air cargo security is the adequacy of cargo inspection procedures and oversight of cargo inspections at air carrier and freight forwarder facilities. The debate over explosives screening of cargo has been around for more than ten years, but was significantly intensified following the 9/11 attacks. In 1997, the Gore Commission recommended that unaccompanied express packages shipped on commercial passenger aircraft should be subject to examination by explosives detection systems.[43] Following the 9/11 attacks, ATSA established a requirement for screening and inspection of all individuals, goods, property, vehicles, and other equipment entering a secured area of a passenger airport. This requirement mandated the same level of protection as passenger and baggage screening, but did not explicitly require the use of any specific screening technologies or techniques.

ATSA did not establish specific requirements for the physical screening of air cargo. With regard to air cargo, current regulations specify that aircraft operators must use the procedures, facilities, and equipment described in their security program to prevent or deter the carriage of unauthorized explosives or incendiaries in cargo onboard a passenger aircraft and inspect cargo shipments for such devices before it is loaded onto passenger aircraft. With regard to all-cargo aircraft, ATSA mandates that a system to screen, inspect, or otherwise ensure the security of all-cargo aircraft is to be established as soon as practicable, but sets no specific deadlines or time frame for compliance. Additionally, aircraft operators must establish controls over cargo shipments, in accordance with their security program, that prevent the carriage of unauthorized explosive or incendiary devices aboard passenger aircraft and access by unauthorized individuals. Further, aircraft operators must refuse to transport any cargo presented by a shipper that refuses to consent to a search and inspection of their shipment.[44]

The Homeland Security Appropriations Act of 2005 (P.L. 108-334) called for tripling the amount of cargo placed on passenger airplanes that is screened or inspected; however the absolute number or percentage of cargo subject to inspection is considered security sensitive. FY2006 appropriations language (P.L. 109-90) directed the TSA to take all possible measures — including the certification, procurement, and deployment of screening systems — to inspect and screen air cargo on passenger aircraft and increase the percentage of cargo inspected beyond the level mandated in the FY2005 appropriations measure. Further, FY2007 appropriations language (P.L. 109-295) directed the TSA to work with industry stakeholders to develop standards and protocols to increase the use of explosives detection equipment for screening air cargo. Similarly the FY2008 Omnibus Appropriations Act (P.L. 110-161) directed the DHS to research, develop, and procure new technologies to screen air cargo, and in the interim utilize checked baggage explosives detection equipment to the maximum extent practicable to screen air cargo placed on passenger aircraft.

While the TSA has taken steps to increase physical inspections of cargo carried aboard passenger aircraft, 100% screening of all cargo placed on passenger aircraft remains a challenge. In August 2007, the Implementing the 9/11 Commission Recommendations Act of 2007 (P.L. 110-53) was enacted. Air cargo screening was a contentious issue during the legislative debate. In the end, the act included a provision requiring 100% physical screening and inspection of all cargo placed on passenger aircraft by August 2010, with an interim requirement to screen 50% of such cargo by February 2009. The act identifies specific methods of screening that would be acceptable in meeting this requirement, including the use of x-ray systems, explosives detection systems, explosives trace detection, TSA-certified explosives detection canine teams, and physical searches conducted in conjunction with manifest verifications. Additional methods may be approved by the TSA. However, the provision specifically prohibits the use of cargo documents and known shipper verification by themselves as being acceptable screening methods. Language in the FY2008 Omnibus Appropriations Act requires the TSA to continually increase the percent of passenger air cargo that is screened, and provide Congress with quarterly updates on the progress being made toward achieving 100% screening of all cargo placed on passenger aircraft. In January 2008, the Chairman of the House Committee on Homeland Security Bennie Thompson and Representative Ed Markey requested a GAO review of the TSA's approach and progress toward meeting the mandate for 100% screening of passenger air cargo, citing concerns that Congress has limited information regarding the TSA's implementation plans.[45]

During congressional debate, air cargo industry stakeholders voiced considerable opposition to requiring 100% screening of passenger air cargo, urging Congress instead to "... focus on realistic solutions based on a framework that identifies and prioritizes risks, works methodically to apply effective and practical security programs, and makes optimal use of federal and industry resources."[46] The industry has continually advocated for a risk-based screening system for cargo placed on passenger airlines that incorporates threat assessment and targeting capabilities, provides incentives for shippers to strengthen supply chain measures, and focuses increased inspections on cargo determined to be of elevated risk through risk assessment and targeting capabilities. This roughly parallels the TSA's strategic plan for air cargo security, which focuses on risk-based targeted screening of cargo. The industry has specifically recommended increased use of canine explosives detection teams; enhanced supply chain security; enhanced targeting of shipments based on the Customs and Border Protection (CBP) experience with its Automated Targeting System (ATS); expanded use of explosive trace detection (ETD) technology for targeted screening; and accelerated research and development of technologies that can more efficiently inspect elevated risk cargo.[47]

A significant ongoing challenge regarding cargo inspection is the feasibility of implementing inspection procedures that offer adequate assurances for security without unduly affecting cargo shipment schedules and processes. However, many in the air cargo industry have expressed continued concerns that current technology does not offer a readily available, affordable solution for scanning cargo containers or bulk cargo in an expeditious manner that would not unduly affect the schedule of air cargo operations. Also, scanning or inspecting individual packages is considered infeasible by many experts due to the volume of cargo handled and the schedule demands of the air cargo business. Therefore, most experts have maintained that the most practical solution, using available technology, is the application of physical screening and inspections on selected shipments and the use of cargo profiling procedures such as known shipper programs coupled with canine explosives detection teams to identify shipments that may require additional screening and inspection.

The DHS Science and Technology Directorate, in coordination with the TSA, initiated an air cargo screening pilot program at three airports — San Francisco International (SFO), Seattle-Tacoma International (SEA) in FY2006 and Cincinnati/Northern Kentucky International (CVG) in FY2007 — to test technologies and procedures for cargo screening.[48] The tests are looking at a combination of X-ray, explosives detection systems (EDS), and ETD screening technologies to determine the best fit for effectively screening air cargo and optimizing the flow and speed of cargo screening. It is anticipated that the results of these pilot tests will be provided to the TSA in FY2009 to aid in decisions regarding the technology approach to be taken to meet the 100% cargo screening mandate, along with guidance regarding the best insertion point for selected technologies in the supply chain to optimize security and efficiency. Additional research will focus on capabilities to better detect, and also to disable, improvised explosive devices (IEDs) in cargo.

Canine Explosives Detection Teams

Since the ability to screen and inspect cargo may be limited to some degree by available technology, flight schedules, and cargo processing demands, alternative measures for screening and inspection at cargo handling facilities have been suggested. The use of canine explosives detection teams has long been suggested as a possible means for screening cargo for explosives. In 1997, the Gore Commission recommended a significant expansion of the use of bomb-sniffing dogs. Similarly, as Congress began looking at options for addressing concerns over explosives placed in air cargo in 2003, former TSA head, Admiral James Loy, testified that increased use of canine teams may be an effective means for increasing inspections of cargo and mail.[49] Canine teams may offer a viable alternative means for screening air cargo at a relatively low cost. As previously noted, air cargo industry stakeholders are presently advocating the increased use of explosives detection canine teams as an integral part of a risk-based approach to air cargo targeting and screening. However, some believe that adequate assurances regarding the security of cargo placed upon passenger aircraft cannot be provided without 100% physical screening predominantly relying on explosives detection technology, as is currently required for all checked baggage.

Supplemental appropriations provided in FY2007 (see P.L. 110-28) provided a total of $80 million for air cargo, to be expended through FY2008, to carry out a variety of air cargo security initiatives including increasing the number of canine teams in the National Explosives Detection Canine Program by at least 170 new teams. All totaled, this will bring the number of TSA canine teams covering all transportation modes to about 600. A large percentage of these teams are involved in passenger air cargo screening activities. Also, the TSA is working with the DHS Science and Technology Directorate to study training techniques and operational procedures to improve canine detection capabilities. One technology being examined is Remote Air Sampling Canine Olfaction (RASCO) sensors, which can provide a concentrated sample from a container for a canine to inspect and has been used extensively in Europe.[50] The DHS project plans to expand this concept to include chemical sensors carried on jackets worn by the canine that will be capable of transmitting data to remote monitoring stations. This appears to address a provision in the FY2007 supplemental appropriations language directing the TSA to "pursue canine screening methods utilized internationally that focus on air samples."[51]

The Cost of Cargo Screening and Inspection

Despite considerable public policy discussion regarding the physical screening of air cargo placed on passenger airliners, there is relatively limited information regarding the estimated cost of carrying out proposals to conduct physical screening of 100% of cargo carried on passenger aircraft. This is, in part, attributable to the fact that there is not yet an agreed upon approach to meeting this mandate. It remains uncertain what role various technologies, such as X-ray, EDS, and ETD, along with canine explosives detection teams will play in meeting this requirement. A statement attributed to David Wirsing, Executive Director of the Airforwarders Association, asserted that implementing this proposal would cost "over $700 million in the first year alone."[52]

The TSA has not publicly disclosed a formal cost estimate for screening all cargo placed on passenger aircraft. However, a statement attributed to TSA spokeswoman Andrea McCauley, indicated that screening cargo placed only on passenger aircraft "would cost an estimated $3.6 billion over 10 years."[53] CRS analyzed the cost to screen all cargo carried on passenger aircraft. This analysis was based on a comparison to costs incurred to meet the mandate for 100% baggage screening and a comparison of the annual volume of cargo carried on passenger aircraft to the estimated annual volume of checked baggage. This approach yielded a ten-year estimate of roughly $3.75 billion for meeting the proposed mandate to screen 100% of cargo placed on passenger aircraft, roughly in line with the estimate attributed to the TSA. However, additional complexities associated with air cargo, such as large sized and irregular shaped shipments, that were not taken into account in this analysis could further increase estimated costs by making the screening process more labor intensive, or by requiring the additional deployment of alternative technologies for screening. These and other factors may explain the larger anticipated initial year costs estimated by the Airforwarders Association, reflected in their estimate of $700 million in the first year of 100% screening. While these factors have generally been acknowledged by industry experts, it has not been fully determined how these unique factors may affect the overall cost of screening cargo. On the other hand, through leveraging technology development and applying operational efficiencies developed from experience with baggage screening as well as the ongoing air cargo screening pilot tests, the total cost of implementing cargo screening may be reduced to some degree.

The Congressional Budget Office (CBO), nonetheless, provided a somewhat higher cost estimate, indicating that it might cost $250 million in the first year and $650 million per year for the following five years, for a total of $3.5 billion over six years, to implement the mandate for 100% baggage screening.[54] The CBO, however, did not provide any specific details regarding how it arrived at this estimate. The CBO also noted that the insufficient information was available to determine whether this new mandate would impose costs on private-sector entities. With regard to who will carry out the mandated cargo screening and who will pay, P.L. 110-53 does not provide clear guidance. Therefore, it remains uncertain whether some or all of the costs for mandated cargo screening will be included in the TSA budget, or how much will have to be covered by the air cargo industry.

Regarding the costs for screening cargo, the potential for additional fees is a particular concern for air cargo industry stakeholders. While P.L. 110-53 included the mandate for 100% cargo screening, it did not include any provisions to establish air cargo security fees or identify any other new revenue sources to pay for this mandate. During legislative debate, House majority leadership has indicated that it would not propose new deficit spending to pay for cargo screening, and that "...airlines would be expected to pay for air cargo inspections."[55] Under such a scheme, it would be most likely that physical screening of air cargo would become an air carrier responsibility with TSA oversight to insure regulatory compliance. Under such an arrangement, airlines would incur the direct costs for meeting the 100% screening requirements. However, more recently House Homeland Security Chairman Bennie Thompson and House Transportation and Infrastructure Committee Chairman Jerry Costello both made statements indicating that cargo screening should be a government responsibility, and that it was the intent of the legislation to have federal employees carrying out the cargo screening required under this mandate.[56]

The act, however, does not specify who is to conduct the screening, and the TSA has interpreted the language to allow airlines, freight forwarders, or even possibly shippers and manufacturers to conduct the screening so long as they can assure the security of the shipment through the supply chain until it is loaded onto an aircraft.[57]

The TSA maintains that this is the only viable means for meeting the mandate, as the TSA does not currently have the resources to screen the volume of cargo placed on passenger aircraft, and such an inflexible approach would slow the flow of air cargo.

The TSA remains confident that, so long as a flexible approach is permitted, it will meet the August 2010 deadline for 100% screening, noting that at several smaller airports, the requirement is already being met.58 Under such an approach, it is likely that much of the operational costs associated with cargo screening and inspection will be borne by industry, including airlines, freight forwarders and shippers. The extent to which these screening costs can be absorbed by passing them along to shippers and consumers may be a particular issue of interest, particularly as airlines continue to deal with other rising costs, especially increased fuel costs.

Besides the impact of direct costs for screening, passenger airlines may be competitively disadvantaged compared to all-cargo airlines if these new mandates are implemented. Industry stakeholders have expressed concerns that additional security screening requirements could slow shipments on passenger aircraft, and certain routes may no longer be profitable if cargo revenues are reduced or eliminated as a result of new screening requirements.[59] Given that profit margins for most passenger airlines are relatively small, and most large passenger airlines have failed to achieve any consistent profitability in recent years, the additional burden of both direct and indirect costs associated with a mandate to screen all cargo placed on passenger aircraft may present particular fiscal challenges to the airlines. While estimated cargo revenues of about $4.7 billion[60] annually make up only about 5% of total industry-wide operating revenues among passenger air carriers, these additional revenues can make the difference between profit or loss in an industry that has seen net losses averaging 3.8% of total revenue during the period from 2003 through 2005, and saw a profit margin of just 1.9% in 2006, the first profitable year for the industry since 2000, when it similarly realized a 1.9% profit margin.[61]

U.S. Mail Carried on Aircraft

The transport of U.S. mail aboard aircraft introduces unique security challenges to prevent illegal hazardous material shipments and the introduction of explosive and incendiary devices. Inspecting first class, priority, and express mail prior to shipment by air is difficult because the

Postal Service regards these items as private materials protected by the Fourth Amendment against search.[62] The Postal Service had implemented a screening process to prevent unauthorized shipments of hazardous substances that relies on customer screening by postal clerks who are trained to question individuals shipping packages weighing more than one pound by air. Following the September 11, 2001 terrorist attacks, however, mail weighing more than one pound was prohibited from being carried aboard passenger aircraft. As seen in Figure 3, there has been a precipitous decline in mail shipments by passenger airlines as a result of this restriction. While all-cargo air carriers have increased their mail carriage to some degree in response, most of the mail once carried aboard passenger aircraft is now being transported by other modes.

Items weighing less than one pound are not subject to any inquiry and can be deposited in mailboxes thereby precluding any questioning or screening of the sender. While these mail items may be shipped on passenger aircraft, only a relatively small percentage of U.S. mail is shipped by air. About 5 to 7.5 percent of all domestic mail shipments, regardless of weight, are transported by either passenger or all-cargo aircraft, and the amount of mail transported on aircraft has declined considerably since the prohibitions following the 9/11 terrorist attacks were put in place. Passenger air carriers have been pushing to have these restrictions lifted because of a significant loss of revenue from U.S. mail shipments. Federal Express is currently the largest carrier of U.S. mail and its all-cargo operations account for about half of the total volume of U.S. mail shipments by air.[63]

In 1997, the Gore Commission had recommended that the Postal Service obtain authorization from customers shipping mail weighing more than one pound allowing screening of shipments using explosive detection systems, and if necessary, seek appropriate legislation to accomplish this.[64] However, this recommendation has never been implemented, and physical inspection of mail shipments is still generally prohibited.

Canine teams, which have been advocated by industry for increased use in screening and inspecting air freight, have provided the only means approved by the TSA for screening mail weighing more than one pound that is put on passenger aircraft under a pilot program conducted at 11 airports.[65] Despite indications that the pilot program worked well, the TSA has not announced any plans to expand the use of canine teams or relax restrictions on air mail shipments.

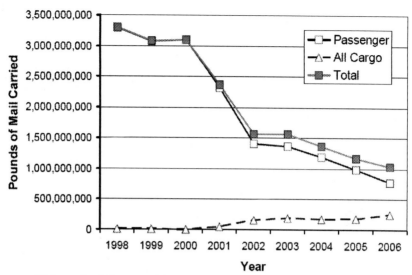

Source: CRS graph of Bureau of Transportation Statistics, Air Carrier T-100 Market Data.

Figure 4. Domestic Air Mail Enplaned (1998-2006).

Assuring the safety and security of U.S. mail transported by aircraft, and preventing the introduction of explosives or incendiaries in mail shipped by aircraft while maintaining privacy rights of postal patrons remains an important issue in the larger debate over air cargo security, although experts don't expect any significant changes to the restrictions on mail greater than one pound anytime soon.. Following the events of September 11, 2001 and the Postal Service anthrax incidents, the Technology Subcommittee of the President's Commission on the United States Postal Service recommended that the Postal Service, in coordination with the Department of Homeland Security, should explore technologies and procedures for utilizing unique sender identification on all mail.[66] While such procedures may provide a means of pre-screening all mail shipped by air, including packages weighing less than one pound, they introduce considerable concerns over the privacy of citizens using the U.S. mail system. Despite considerable policy discussion of implementing unique sender identification, and possibly mail tracking technologies as well, in the aftermath of the 2001 anthrax attacks, implementing these capabilities for all types of mail presents considerable legal and logistic challenges that are yet to be resolved.

PHYSICAL SECURITY OF AIR CARGO FACILITIES

Air cargo facilities present unique challenges for physical security. The large physical size of these facilities and relatively continuous high-volume cargo operations introduce numerous individuals, vehicles, and shipments into secured access areas around aircraft. Key issues regarding physical security of these air cargo facilities include the adequacy of

- inspections and oversight of air cargo facilities to ensure compliance with aviation security regulations and procedures established in the approved security programs of air carriers and freight forwarders;
- training for air cargo personnel with regard to security procedures and guidelines; and
- access control requirements for personnel with access to air cargo facilities and aircraft.

These issues are presently being addressed through newly implemented air cargo security regulations issued by the TSA in May 2006 that are currently being implemented at air carrier and freight forwarder operations and logistics facilities.[67]

Congressional oversight of industry implementation and compliance with these regulations may, therefore, continue to be an issue of particular interest during the 110th Congress.

Inspection and Oversightof Air Cargo Facilities

Current regulations specify that all air carriers and freight forwarders must allow the TSA to conduct inspections and to review and copy records in order to determine compliance with applicable laws and regulations pertaining to aviation security. The Homeland Security Appropriations Act for FY2005 provided the TSA with $40 million to hire an additional 100 inspectors to carry out oversight and enforcement activities related to air cargo security. The TSA has responded by launching focused inspections of air cargo operations and conducting monthly "blitz" audits or "strikes" of selected air cargo facilities. In FY2006, Congress again provided the TSA with a $10 million set-aside to hire 100 more air cargo inspectors and for travel related to carrying out regulatory oversight and inspections of air cargo shipping and handling facilities, but the TSA has been slow to obligate these funds for air cargo security. For FY2007, appropriations report language directed the TSA to hire additional permanent staff to enhance TSA's analytic air cargo security capabilities.[68] In addition, an FY2007 supplemental appropriation (see P.L. 110-28) totaling $80 million was provided for air cargo security activities, including the hiring of an additional 150 compliance inspectors and cargo vulnerability assessments at the nation's busiest airports (i.e., Category X airports). Similarly, increased funding for air cargo security in FY2008 appropriations was provided for the hiring of additional air cargo inspectors and reducing reliance on contractors to carry out regulatory compliance activities related to air cargo security.

Increased oversight of air cargo facilities is likely to be highly dependent on the continued availability of resources and funding. The effectiveness of this oversight will also likely be highly dependent on the adequacy of available tools and procedures to track needed corrective actions and ensure compliance among air carriers and freight forwarders. Therefore, the adequacy of TSA's oversight of air cargo security could be a significant area of focus for congressional oversight during the 110th Congress.

Cargo Security Training

Currently, air cargo handlers are not required to receive any specific or formal training on security procedures or identification of suspicious activities. However, air cargo handlers may be considered the front line in protecting against security threats by adhering to procedures that would mitigate physical security breaches at cargo operations facilities, by increasing their awareness of suspicious activities, and by following proper procedures for reporting their observations. Security training for cargo workers may focus on security procedures for ensuring cargo integrity, protecting facilities, reporting suspicious activities, and so on. Under the TSA regulations imposed in 2006, workers for all-cargo carriers and for indirect air carriers with security-related duties — such as carrying out security inspections of shipments — are now required to receive specific training on the company's security program and their individual security-related responsibilities under that program. Similar training is already required of workers for passenger airlines that are assigned security-related duties.

Increased Control over Access to Aircraft and Cargo Facilities

Under ATSA, TSA was directed to work with airport operators to strengthen access control points in secured areas and was authorized to use biometric screening procedures to positively identify individuals with access to secure airport areas.

ATSA contains provisions for TSA oversight of secured-area access control to assess and enforce compliance with access control requirements. These requirements include screening and inspection of individuals, goods, property, vehicles and other equipment seeking to access secure airport areas. Background checks for individuals having access to passenger aircraft are required and vendors with direct access to airfields where passenger operations take place are required to have a TSA-approved security program in place. Presently, background checks and displayed identification serve as the principal means for screening airport workers including cargo handlers.

There has been growing concern over the adequacy of these procedures for screening and monitoring airport workers. One particular concern is the integrity of airport worker credentials and the potential that unauthorized individuals could gain access to secure areas of the airport using stolen or fraudulent identification. The TSA has begun to implement a universal biometric Transportation Workers Identification Credential (TWIC) for the nation's seaports. Biometric technology has received considerable attention from Congress as a means to authenticate individuals, particularly airport workers, and improve access controls to secured areas of airports.

While it is not expected that the TSA will incorporate airports into the TWIC program, it has been moving forward in developing specific guidelines for airports to incorporate biometrics into their airport credentialing and access control systems.

These proposals are discussed in further detail below in the section titled "Biometric Screening Technology."

Another concern has been raised over the use of identification checks in lieu of physical screening of airport workers, including cargo handlers. Representative Peter DeFazio, for example, has expressed concern over this practice noting that workers who bypass physical screening could potentially carry threat objects into secured areas of the airport or on board aircraft.[69] These concerns were again raised in 2007 when airline workers in Orlando were arrested after using their airport access credentials to bypass security checkpoints and smuggle weapons on flights to Puerto Rico.[70] Congress may consider whether existing security procedures regarding airport worker access to secured airport areas meets the intent of ATSA with regard to providing at least the same level of protection of secured airport areas and passenger aircraft as screening passengers and their baggage. The FY2008 Consolidated Appropriations Act (P.L. 110-161) provides funding to the TSA to carry out a pilot program to assess physical screening of airport employees. The TSA intends to study the costs and risks associated with various full screening and random screening protocols for airport workers.

In addition to ongoing concerns over access controls around passenger aircraft, access control and monitoring of workers at all-cargo facilities remains a significant challenge. Regulations promulgated in 2006 establish an all-cargo security program detailing the physical security measures for air cargo operations areas, cargo placed aboard all-cargo aircraft, and background checks and screening of individuals having access to their aircraft on the ground or in flight. In addition, these new air cargo security rules require airports to designate cargo operations areas, including areas where all-cargo aircraft are loaded and unloaded, as security identification display areas (SIDAs). This effectively elevates the required security measures for these cargo handling areas and requires that workers with unescorted access to these areas be vetted through fingerprint-based criminal history records checks (CHRCs), as has been required for workers having access to secured areas around passenger aircraft for some time.

Arming All-Cargo Pilots

During the 108th Congress, proponents for arming all-cargo pilots urged Congress to allow all-cargo pilots to join the ranks of passenger airline pilots who can volunteer for selection and training in the Federal Flight Deck Officers (FFDO) program. This program, established by the Homeland Security Act of 2002 (P.L. 107-296), trains and deputizes qualified pilots to carry firearms and use deadly force to protect the flight deck against terrorist attacks While the plan was originally limited to only pilots of passenger airliners, Vision 100 (P.L. 108-176) expanded the program to allow all-cargo pilots and flight engineers to participate as well.

Proponents for including all-cargo pilots in the program point out that all-cargo aircraft lack hardened cockpit doors, federal air marshals, and passengers that may assist in thwarting a hijacking attempt.[71] They also point out that physical security and access control to cargo operations areas and all-cargo aircraft had not been held to the same standard as passenger airline operations prior to the implementation of tougher regulations for air cargo security. Proponents for arming all-cargo pilots also point out that the lack of screening of individuals and property at air cargo facilities could offer the opportunity for terrorists plotting to hijack an aircraft to board an allcargo aircraft as stowaways and seize the cockpit in flight. All-cargo aircraft include more than 1,000 transport category jet airplanes, of which about half are widebody jets similar to those used in the September 11, 2001 terrorist attacks.[72] Proponents for arming all-cargo pilots contend that the provision in Vision 100 that includes cargo pilots in the FFDO program will mitigate the risk of a hijacking aboard allcargo aircraft. They further argue that training for cargo pilots is needed expediently given the limited measures currently in place to mitigate this risk.

Cargo airlines, on the other hand, had opposed allowing their pilots to join the FFDO program. Air carriers, in general, have been hesitant about the program because of liability concerns even though specific liability protections were extended to the airlines and pilot participants when the FFDO program was established under the Homeland Security Act of 2002 (P.L. 107-296). Proponents for the program and the inclusion of cargo pilots in the program have voiced concerns that the manner in which the program has been implemented and the remoteness of the training facilities have limited the program's overall effectiveness. The program, along with other flight crew security training initiatives, has received annual appropriations of about $25 million since it was fully implemented in FY2004. Few, if any, changes to the program are expected in the near term. Nonetheless, Congress may at some point address some lingering concerns over the program such as the convenience of training and requalification sites, the carriage of firearms outside the cockpit, which is presently highly restricted, and program liability surrounding the role of the federal flight deck officer as both an airline pilot and a deputized federal officer.

TECHNOLOGY FOR AIR CARGO SECURITY

Because the capability of available technology is seen as a significant constraining factor on the ability to screen, inspect, and track cargo, initiatives to improve cargo screening technology have been a focus of recent legislation to enhance air cargo security.

In response to the 9/11 Commission recommendation that the TSA intensify its efforts to identify, track, and appropriately screen potentially dangerous cargo, the National Intelligence Reform Act of 2004 (P.L. 108-458) directed the TSA to develop technologies for this purpose and authorized $100 million annually in FY2005 through FY2007 for the research, development, and deployment of enhanced air cargo security technology. The act also established a competitive grant program to foster the development of advanced air cargo security technology.

Appropriations for research and development of technologies specifically tailored for air cargo security thereafter increased significantly, totaling $55 million in FY2004 and $75 million for FY2005. In FY2006, TSA research and development functions were realigned into the Department of Homeland Security's Science and Technology Directorate and research and development funding for air cargo wasscaled back to $30 million, and specifically designated for conducting three cargo screening pilot programs testing different concepts of operation. In FY2007, the aviation security research and development functions were realigned within the TSA and appropriated a total of $92 million. The appropriations measure did not specify what portion of this would be allocated to air cargo-related research and development, but did urge the TSA to work with industry stakeholders to develop standards and protocols to increase the use of explosives detection equipment for screening air cargo.

Various technologies are under consideration for enhancing the security of air cargo operations. Tamper-evident and tamper resistant packaging and container seals may offer a relatively low cost means of protecting cargo integrity during shipping and handling. Cargo screening technology using X-rays, including X-ray backscatter systems, chemical element sensing ETD systems, computed tomography (CT) scanbased EDS, or possibly neutron beams or other techniques, such as millimeter wave imaging systems, may offer various means to screen cargo prior to placement aboard aircraft. Additionally, canine teams may be used to augment cargo screening technology or to screen cargo independently. Hardened cargo container technology may be used to mitigate the threat of in-flight explosions or incendiary fires aboard aircraft. Finally, biometric technologies are being evaluated and may be useful in authenticating cargo worker identification and improving access control to aircraft and cargo operations areas.

Tamper-Evidentand Tamper-Resistant Seals

Various technologies exist for sealing cargo shipments and cargo containers to prevent tampering.

Relatively low cost solutions such as tamper-evident tapes that provide visual indications of tampering are readily available and could easily be implemented during packaging. Such technology could be used in combination with "known shipper" protocols to insure that known shippers provide sufficient security in their packaging facilities and to deter tampering and theft during shipping and handling. Tamperevident tape can identify cargo during inspections processes for further screening and inspection to safeguard against the introduction of explosives and incendiary devices.

Tamper-evident tape may also be an effective tool to deter cargo crime, including cargo theft and the introduction of contraband, counterfeit, and pirated goods during shipment.

At cargo handling facilities, tamper evident seals and locks can be utilized on cargo containers to prevent theft and the introduction of contraband or threat objects into air cargo shipments. Electronic seals may serve as an additional deterrent to terrorist and criminal activity by providing more immediate detection of tampering.

Electronic seals have alarms, some triggered by fiber optic cable loops, that activate a transmitted signal when tampered with.[73] Electronic seals cost about $2,500 per unit, but are reusable. However, the utility of electronic seals in air cargo operations has been questioned by some experts because currently available electronic seals have a limited transmission range, which may make detecting and identifying seals that have been tampered with difficult. In addition, there is some concern that they may interfere with aircraft electronic systems.[74]

In addition to tamper-evident and tamper-resistant seals, technologies to better track cargo shipments are being considered to maintain better control and tracking of cargo shipments along the supply chain. Both global positioning system (GPS) and radio-frequency identification (RFID) technologies are seen as emerging technologies for improving the tracking of air cargo in the supply chain.

Cargo Screening Technology

Various technologies are available for detecting explosives, incendiary devices, and the presence of various chemical and biological agents and nuclear weapons in cargo. Key technologies under consideration for screening air cargo for threat objects include X-ray screening, CT scan-based explosive detection systems (EDS), chemical explosives trace detection (ETD) systems, and technologies based on neutron beams. Newer technologies under consideration for screening passengers at screening checkpoints, including Xray backscatter and millimeter wave imaging technologies have the capability to penetrate various cargo container materials, and thus may also be adaptable for use in air cargo screening. In addition to these technological approaches, several experts and TSA officials have been advocating and pursuing an increased use of canine teams for screening cargo and mail. The main drawback to any of these screening techniques is that the screening process takes time and may significantly impact cargo delivery schedules. Another concern regarding these technologies is the cost associated with acquisition, operation, and maintenance of screening systems.

X-Ray Screening

The most common systems currently available for largescale screening of cargo shipments utilize X-ray technology. These systems rely on well understood transmission and backscatter X-ray techniques to probe cargo containers. Many of these systems utilize low-dose X-ray sources that emit narrow X-ray beams thus virtually eliminating the need for shielding. These devices are compact and light weight, thus allowing them to be mounted on moving platforms that can scan over containers.[75] X-ray devices are becoming more common at major ports of entry, border crossings, and airports overseas as post-September 11th security concerns are spurring increased development and deployment of these devices. The systems are also being utilized to screen for drugs and other contraband as well as explosives in cargo shipments.

In addition to traditional X-ray systems, X-ray backscatter technology, which measures the scatter or reflections of the X-ray beam. The X-ray backscatter technology tends to do a much better job of differentiating organic materials because different chemical elements in these materials scatter the X-ray in quite different patterns. This makes X-ray backscatter a well suited technology for detecting organic explosives in either solid or liquid form. However, like traditional X-ray technology, current X-ray backscatter systems are extremely labor intensive and require considerable staffing and training requirements because these systems require human operators to control the system and interpret the backscatter images.

One of the most significant operational challenges in using X-ray screening devices, whether they be traditional X-ray systems or newer X-ray backscatter technologies, is the performance of the human operator. A variety of human factors considerations contribute to the operator's ability to detect threat objects when viewing X-ray images. These include the monotony of the task, fatigue, time pressure, the adequacy of training, and working conditions. These human factors are important to consider in fielding X-ray screening systems to ensure high detection rates of threat objects while minimizing false alarm rates that would unnecessarily slow the cargo inspection and handling process. Technologies such as threat image projection (TIP), that superimpose stored images of threat objects on X-ray scans can help keep operators alert and may be effective tools for training and performance monitoring. Additional technologies, such as computer algorithms for highlighting potential threat objects, may also be considered to aid human observers.

Explosive Detection Systems (EDS)

Currently, EDS technologies are being used extensively in the aviation security environment, particularly in response to the mandate in ATSA requiring screening of all checked passenger baggage by EDS. These systems use X-ray computed tomography to scan objects, and computational algorithms that assess the probability of threat object detection based on object density characteristics. Certified EDS systems must meet acceptable detection and false alarm rates for bulk explosives detection. While most specific performance criteria of certified EDS systems are classified, EDS systems used for passenger checked baggage must meet or exceed a throughput rate of 450 bags per hour.

The TSA has gained considerable experience with the large scale deployment and use of EDS equipment to meet the mandate for full explosives detection screening of checked passenger bags. Many of the lessons learned by TSA from this experience will be useful for assessing the technical and operational challenges of applying large-scale EDS screening initiatives for air cargo operations. Efforts are also underway at TSA to improve the performance of EDS equipment and reduce its cost. However, air cargo operations are likely to present some of their own unique challenges for implementing large scale EDS screening of freight, express packages, and mail. Some of the potential operational challenges associated with effectively fielding existing EDS equipment for screening air cargo include

- the limited size of objects that can be placed in EDS machines, which would require objects to be screened before being placed in containers or on pallets;
- the distributed nature of the air cargo system often involves loading containers at remote sites, and EDS screening at these remote sites may leave the system vulnerable to possible introduction of explosives or incendiary devices at points along the supply chain beyond the screening site;
- reported high false alarm rates of current generation EDS systems may lead to high levels of secondary screening and detailed inspections that could impact the ability to meet the schedule demands of cargo operations; and
- the processing rate of EDS equipment may require the purchase of large numbers of EDS machines and investment in the research and development of alternative technologies, thus increasing program costs, to minimize the impact on cargo operations scheduling and meet desired security program goals, although the throughput of EDS equipment has markedly improved over the last few years.

Chemical Trace Detection Systems

Chemical trace detection systems, referred to commonly as ETD devices are being widely used as secondary screening tools for passenger carry-on and checked baggage. Items identified for closer scrutiny by initial screening methods or selected at random may undergo further .examination using these systems. These systems use a variety of technical principles to analyze the chemical composition of sample residue wiped from suspect articles.

These systems compare the chemical composition of such a sample to the signature of known explosive materials and signal an alarm to the operator if the probability of a match exceeds a specified threshold.

The use of chemical trace detection systems is now common practice in the screening of checked and carry-on bags. It has been reported that TSA is considering expanding the use of chemical trace detection systems for screening cargo carried aboard passenger aircraft.[76] However, screening procedures using these systems are very labor intensive and time consuming. Like the manner in which this technology is used to perform secondary screening of checked and carry on bags, chemical trace detection may be employed in air cargo operations to perform detailed screening of suspicious packages identified through known shipper databases, or can be used for detailed secondary screening in conjunction with primary screening performed by Xray and EDS systems similar to procedures currently in use for checked baggage screening. Random screening of cargo using chemical trace detection systems as a primary screening method is unlikely to be effective given the very low percentage of cargo that could be screened using this technique without significantly impacting cargo operations schedules. However, using chemical trace detection systems in conjunction with canine teams as a secondary screening tool appears to provide a possible option for increasing the proportion of cargo that can be effectively screened in a time efficient manner.

Neutron Beam Technologies

Another potential class of technologies for screening air cargo is based on neutron beams. These systems use a pulsed neutron generator to probe an object, initiating several low energy nuclear reactions with the chemical elements comprising the object. Detectors can then measure the nuclear signature of the transmitted neutrons and/or the gamma-rays emitted from the reactions. Since neutrons and gamma-rays have the ability to penetrate through various materials to large depths in a non-intrusive manner, neutron technologies may have advantages for cargo screening, and some of these technologies are currently being operationally evaluated for use in contraband and explosives detection.[77] However, the GAO noted that currently available neutron-based technologies cost about $10 million per machine and require about one hour per container for screening thus making this option very expensive and time consuming.[78]

In addition to the cost and time factors associated with neutron beam technologies, the National Research Council (NRC) has raised considerable doubts about performance capabilities for screening the full spectrum of cargo containers or pallets for explosives.[79] The NRC also expressed potential safety concerns over the use of radiation-producing particle accelerators, and expressed concerns over the practicality of using this technology in the aviation environment because of the size and weight of the equipment.

In 1999, the NRC advised the FAA against further funding for research, development, and deployment of a neutron-based explosive detection system known as pulsed fast/thermal neutron spectroscopy (PFTNS) for primary screening of carry-on baggage, checked baggage, or cargo citing low current explosive threat levels and inadequate performance. In 2002, the NRC concluded that another neutron-based technique, pulsed fast neutron analysis (PFNA), is not ready for airport deployment or testing. However, the NRC conceded that PFNA has greater potential for screening containerized cargo than any other technology currently under consideration at the time of their analysis.[80] Since this analysis, however, interest in neutron beam screening technologies has largely taken a back seat to EDS and ETD technologies, as well as other potential screening technologies, including X-ray backscatter and millimeter wave imaging systems. Because the perceived threat of explosives has increased since September 11, 2001, neutron-based detection technology continues to be mentioned as a possible means for screening air cargo.

However, wide-scale deployment of this technology for air cargo security in the near term seems unlikely.

Millimeter Wave Imaging Systems

Millimeter wave screening technology refers to a wide array of screening devices capable of creating highly detailed images by measuring the reflections of ultra high frequency (i.e., in the 30-300 giga-Hertz frequency range) waves emitted by the system that are capable of passing through barriers that normally preclude visual inspection. Millimeter wave imaging systems are capable of penetrating many shipping container materials, and therefore potentially have a broad array of homeland security applications, including the screening of air cargo. While the TSA has been field testing millimeter wave imaging systems for passenger screening that are capable of penetrating clothing to detect concealed weapons and explosives, interest in the use of millimeter wave imaging systems for air cargo screening has been more limited at this point.

Nonetheless, commercial products using millimeter wave imaging are currently available for application in standoff scanning of a wide variety of objects, including cargo, from a distance of several meters.[81] While images from multiple angles are typically required to get a complete picture of a container's contents, currently available millimeter wave imaging systems are capable of generating relatively high detail images of items held inside a cargo container. However, like X-ray screening technologies, millimeter wave imaging systems are labor intensive, and can be expensive to operate, because they require trained operators to interpret the images generated by the system and identify potential threats for further examination. While interest in millimeter wave technology for air cargo screening has thus far been somewhat limited, interest in this technology may be intensified by new screening requirements and searches for efficient technologies to meet the mandate for 100% screening of cargo placed on passenger airliners.

Blast-Resistant Cargo Containers

In addition to cargo screening technology, hardened cargo container technology is being considered as a means to mitigate the threat of an explosion or fire caused by a bomb or incendiary device that makes its way onto an aircraft undetected. The 9/11 Commission formally recommended the deployment of at least one hardened cargo container on every passenger aircraft that also hauls cargo to carry suspicious cargo. The National Intelligence Reform Act of 2004 (P.L. 108-248) requires the TSA to establish a pilot program to explore the feasibility of this concept and authorizes the use of incentives to airlines to offset added fuel, maintenance, and other operational costs associated with using hardened cargo containers in an effort to encourage voluntary participation in the pilot program. The act authorized $2 million for the pilot program. A provision in the Implementing the 9/11 Commission Recommendations Act of 2007 (P.L. 110-53) directed the TSA to provide an evaluation of the pilot program and, based on its findings, implement a program to pay for, provide, and maintain blastresistant cargo containers for use by air carriers on a risk-managed basis.

This concept of deploying hardened cargo containers has been a topic of ongoing research for some time. Following the December 21, 1988 bombing of Pan Am flight 103 over Lockerbie, Scotland, the British Air Accident Investigation Branch recommended that regulatory authorities and airplane manufacturers study methods to mitigate the effects of in-flight explosions.[82] The FAA has had a active research program in blast-resistant containers for more than 10 years examining the airworthiness, ground handling, and blast resistance of hardened containers, which is now overseen by the TSA's Transportation Security Laboratory. These containers, or hardened unit-loading devices (HULDs), are seen as a potential means for mitigating the threat of explosives placed aboard passenger aircraft in either checked baggage or cargo. These containers must withhold an explosive blast of a specified magnitude without any rupturing or fragment penetration of the container wall or the aircraft structure, and must contain and "self-extinguish" any post-blast fire in order to meet the FAA-established test criteria.[83]

However, the increased weight of these containers could have significant operational impacts on airlines by increasing fuel costs and decreasing payload capacity for carrying revenue passengers and cargo. Challenges associated with deploying hardened cargo containers include

- increased weight affecting aircraft range and payload capacity;
- increased procurement cost for hardened containers;
- potentially higher maintenance costs for hardened container materials;
- potential reduction in cargo volume (in addition to reduced payload weight) due to thicker container walls; and
- possible design specifications, such as door hinging and positioning, that are not compatible with current airline baggage and cargo loading procedures and operations facilities.[84]

The National Research Council (NRC) estimated that the per unit cost for acquiring hardened cargo containers would be $10,000, and recommended that the FAA continue efforts to operationally test HULDs and establish more rigorous protocol for certifying HULDs, but should not deploy them unless deemed to be a necessary security measure based on the assessments of cost, operational, and deployment studies by FAA and other stakeholders.

The NRC panel also recommended further economic assessment of their proposed deployment plan for fielding one HULD per wide-body aircraft. The NRC panel also noted that research and development on the use of HULDs on narrowbody aircraft was lagging far behind the work done on wide-body aircraft, and recommended an increased emphasis on research in this area to assess the operational effectiveness of HULDs in narrow-body aircraft before any further recommendations could be made. The NRC panel estimated that the cost of deploying enough HULDS for airlines to carry at least one HULD per passenger flight would require an industry-wide procurement cost of $125 million, and would create an annual industry-wide economic impact of $11 million in increased fuel burn and reduced payload revenue.[85]

Given the recent increase in aviation jet fuel costs, the economic impact would likely be considerably higher than the NRC originally estimated nine years ago.

Recognizing the continued concerns over the cost and weight associated with currently available blast-resistant container technology, the DHS has proposed a new research program in FY2009 to examine the potential of adapting composite container material development efforts for use in air cargo to provide tamper detection and intrusion resistance with possible blast-resistant capabilities.

The recommendation made by the 9/11 Commission also called for the deployment of at least one hardened cargo container on every passenger aircraft for carrying any suspect cargo.[86] This recommendation implies that a cargo prescreening or risk evaluation process such as a known shipper program or the proposed freight assessment system would be used to determine what cargo should be loaded into the hardened container. Presently, ATSA requires shipments from unknown sources to travel on all-cargo aircraft. One strategic objective of the TSA's Air Cargo Strategic Plan is to develop a means for identifying elevated risk cargo through pre-screening.[87] Such a tool would likely be needed to assess risk and determine what cargo should be placed in a hardened container. Besides the need for a pre-screening process, the use of hardened cargo containers is likely to be opposed by the airline industry because of the direct costs of acquiring these units as well as the increased operational cost associated with increased fuel burn and lost payload capacity. The benefits of using hardened cargo containers would likely be highly dependent on the security of the pre-screening process and its ability to detect high risk cargo since the benefits of a hardened container would largely be negated if the pre-screening process could be circumvented by terrorists. A key policy issue that is likely to emerge as the feasibility of hardened cargo containers is further evaluated is the potential implications of allowing suspicious cargo to travel on passenger aircraft even if this cargo is secured in hardened cargo containers. In other words, policymakers may debate what the risks and benefits of loading suspicious cargo on passenger airplanes in hardened cargo containers is as compared to the alternative of offloading this suspicious cargo to all-cargo aircraft.

In any case, under a plan in which only one hardened cargo container is deployed per aircraft, it is likely that only a relatively small fraction of available cargo space will be reinforced. For example, a Boeing 747-400 passenger jet is capable of holding up to 13 full-width, or 26 half-width containers.[88] Thus, providing just one full sized hardened cargo container for a 747-400 would provide reinforcement for less than 10% of the available cargo storage area. While a greater percentage of available cargo space on smaller jets could be protected by hardened containers, any policy regarding the use of just one hardened container per aircraft will likely need to carefully evaluate the criteria and methods for vetting cargo to determine what cargo should be designated for carriage inside these hardened cargo containers.

In addition to hardened cargo containers, the FAA recently proposed rulemaking[89] that would require newly certified aircraft type to have improved fire suppression capabilities in their cargo holds to withstand and suppress a sudden intensive fire from an explosive or incendiary device. Additionally, the proposed rule would require each newly certified aircraft type to include a "least risk bomb location," an accessible location where crewmembers could place a suspected explosive device to minimize the potential for catastrophic damage to the aircraft if the item explodes. The proposal would also require aircraft designers to isolate flight critical systems and maximize separation of systems, to minimize the chances that a bomb detonation would render the aircraft unflyable. However, because these proposals would only be applied to newly certified aircraft types, these changes would not have a substantial operational impact on aviation safety and security for several years.

Biometric Screening Technology

Provisions of ATSA give the TSA authority to use biometric technology to verify the identity of employees entering the secured areas of airports and directed the TSA to review the effectiveness of biometrics systems currently used by airports such as San Francisco International Airport. Available biometric technologies such as fingerprint, retinal scan, and facial pattern recognition are being tested and implemented as part of a variety of transportation security programs, including the Transportation Worker Identification Credential smart cards and readers for access controls at seaports and the Registered Traveler program for airline passengers who voluntarily provide detailed background information in exchange for expedited processing through airport screening checkpoints.

The National Intelligence Reform Act of 2004 (P.L. 108-458) contains extensive provisions requiring the TSA to develop specific guidance for the use of biometric or other technologies for airport access control systems by March 31, 2005. The guidance is to include comprehensive technical and operating system requirements and performance standards for the use of biometric identifier technology in airport access control systems; a list of products and vendors meeting these specifications; and specific procedures for implementing biometric identifier systems; and a discussion of best practices for incorporating biometric identifier technologies into airport access control systems. The act also provides authorization for $20 million for the research and development of advanced biometric technology applications for aviation security. Pilot studies have been conducted to examine methods for incorporating biometrics into airport access control systems. Given the proposed regulatory changes to enhance access controls to all-cargo facilities and improve existing access controls around passenger aircraft, it is likely that the implementation of biometric identifier technology will play an increasingly important role in air cargo security policy.

FUNDING FOR AIR CARGO SECURITY

The cost of air cargo security options are significant to both the Federal government and the air cargo industry. Furthermore, the indirect costs of air cargo security on air cargo operations may pose significant long-term challenges. On the other hand, the potential costs of a terrorist attack, both in terms of the loss of life and property and the long term economic impacts would also be significant but are difficult to predict and quantify. An ongoing debate tied to air cargo appropriations and oversight of aviation security is the amount of physical screening and inspection of air cargo that is needed and achievable and whether risk-based pre-screening tools can provide an adequate means to ensure the security of air cargo by identifying atrisk cargo for targeted physical inspections. Besides the logistic complexities of inspecting large amounts, or 100%, of cargo on passenger flights, many are concerned that the cost of doing so may impose a significant burden on the aviation and air cargo industries.

While federal expenditures on air cargo security measures have been growing over the past two years, these efforts are a relatively small element (about 2%) of TSA's overall operating budget for aviation security. These expenditures could, continue to grow, however, if additional technology and resources are devoted to the tracking and screening of cargo shipments. In contrast to passenger and baggage screening, which are, with few exceptions, the operational responsibility of the TSA, under the current scheme, much of the cost of inspection and screening of cargo is borne by the airlines and shippers, while TSA only maintains oversight responsibility. As previously noted, to meet the mandate of 100% inspections of air cargo, the TSA estimates a cost of more than $650 million in the first year of implementation, and a total cost of roughly $3.6 billion over 10 years, while the CBO estimates these costs to total $3.5 billion over six year, $250 million in the first year and $650 million for the next five years.[90]

Options for Imposing Air Cargo Security Fees

P.L. 110-53 does not include an aviation security fee in connection with its mandate for 100% screening of cargo placed on passenger aircraft. This leaves open funding questions regarding who would be responsible for operationally carrying out the screening, the federal government or industry, and how these screening functions would be funded. As previously noted, the

TSA intends to rely on industry, including the airlines, freight forwarders, and even shippers in some cases, to carry out much of the physical screening of cargo required under this mandate. The specific operational manner in which TSA technologies and canine explosives detection teams will be integrated into this process relying primarily on industry-operated cargo screening remains unclear and clouds the picture regarding funding requirements and funding sources for air cargo screening operations.

However, some past legislative proposals calling for the TSA to physically screen all cargo shipments bound for passenger aircraft incorporated a fee schedule for shippers to cover costs associated with screening cargo transported in passenger aircraft that is similar to the security fees imposed on airline passengers (see H.R. 2455 and H.R. 3798 introduced in the 108th Congress). Imposing a fee on air cargo shipments for security could provide offsetting collections for air cargo security costs incurred by the government, such as the cost of screening technology development and deployment and the training and deployment of canine explosives detection teams. Regardless of how such a fee might be collected — either through fees assessed to air carriers or freight forwarders or through direct fees applied to each shipment — the costs will ultimately be borne by shippers and ultimately passed on to the customers of their products.

The overall impact of such fees on air cargo would ultimately be dependent on the relative cost of the fee. Since air cargo shipments tend to consist of relatively high value goods, it is likely that the relative cost of a security fee in relation to the value of the shipment will be low, which could minimize the economic impact of imposing such a fee. However, if fees applied to air cargo carried on passenger aircraft are higher than fees for transporting that same cargo on all-cargo aircraft, a significant negative impact on passenger air carrier revenues from cargo may result.

Equity in fee collections will likely be an important consideration in assessing if and how air cargo security fees should be collected.

Potential Impact on Manufacturers and other Shippers

Another possible concern over the increased cost of cargo security associated with screening operations and other security enhancements is the potential that these actions will result in increased shipment costs for manufactured goods, particularly costs related to the distribution of time-critical parts. If unit shipping costs rise enough because of security-related costs and fees, it is possible that domestic manufacturing and assembly costs will not be able to remain competitive in a global market. For example, if the costs of shipping time-critical parts from Asia for final assembly in the United States rise because of security-related costs, it may become cost advantageous to manufacture the entire product overseas or within the United States.

In the long term, this could result in a possible loss of manufacturing jobs in the United States, or in some cases, relocation of certain manufacturing facilities to the United States to eliminate dependence on air cargo. For this reason, the economic implications of any proposal to impose security-related fees on air cargo or impose costly security requirements on air cargo operators and shippers will likely need to be carefully evaluated to avoid or minimize any unintended impacts on manufacturers and their suppliers.

Air Cargo Security Appropriations

While Congress continues to debate the needed level of physical screening and inspection of cargo, current appropriations figures are predicated on continuing and expanding the risk-based approach of prescreening cargo and conducting targeted inspections of elevated-risk cargo and increasing random inspections of other shipments. In FY2003, the TSA received $20 million for cargo screening improvements. In FY2004, the TSA was appropriated $30 million for air cargo security operations. Additionally, research and development related to air cargo security was provided an appropriation of $55 million. For FY2005, the Administration recommended flat funding for air cargo, while the House and the Senate agreed to increases to both the air cargo operations and air cargo research and development accounts totaling $115 million. In FY2006, there was a shift in funding, and for the first time, a larger proportion of air cargo security funding was allocated for use in air cargo operations ($55 million) as compared to research and development ($30 million). Also, as previously noted, the FY2006 air cargo research and development funding has been more specifically directed to focus on three pilot projects, reflecting a maturation of air cargo screening technologies and procedures and a migration from purely a research activity to a testable operational concept. In FY2007, base appropriations for air cargo security operations were again set at $55 million. A specific funding amount for air cargo security-related research and development initiatives was not included in the FY2007 appropriations. However, the TSA and the DHS Science and Technology Directorate are continuing their efforts to adopt EDS technologies to the air cargo environment, and the TSA was directed to work with industry stakeholders to develop standards and protocols to increase the use of explosives detection equipment for screening air cargo.

With the start of the 110th Congress, a congressional focus on improving air cargo security resulted in an $80 million supplemental appropriation for air cargo security. This funding was made available through FY2009 and was specifically designated for hiring additional air cargo inspectors, conducting air cargo vulnerability assessments at all Category X airports, training and deploying additional canine teams, pursuing new methods for canine screening based on technologies and approaches used in other countries, and deploying various technologies, such as EDS and ETD, to screen air cargo. For FY2008, $73 million was appropriated for air cargo security, and the DHS estimates that roughly $2.3 million of its $122 million research budget for explosives detection will focus specifically on air cargo screening technologies and practices. Appropriations language directed the TSA to focus on air cargo screening technologies for meeting the 100% passenger air cargo screening requirements of P.L. 110-53, and in the interim utilize existing baggage screening technologies to the greatest extent practicable to screen air cargo shipments placed on passenger aircraft. For FY2009 the President's Budget Request seeks $86.3 million to continue ongoing initiatives for cargo screening, increase covert testing and inspections of air cargo operations, and develop a certified shipper program to enhance supply chain security. Also, the DHS S&T Directorate requests $3.5 million to continue air cargo and canine explosives detection projects under the air cargo security component of its explosives detection research thrust area.

End Notes

[1] CRS calculations based on Bureau of Transportation Statistics, *Air Carrier Statistics (Form 41 Traffic)*.

[2] Bureau of Transportation Statistics. *Freight In America: A New National Picture*. January, 2006. Washington, DC: U.S. Department of Transportation.

[3] Bureau of Transportation Statistics. *Pocket Guide to Transportation, 2007*. Washington, DC: U.S. Department of Transportation.

[4] *Ibid.*

[5] Bureau of Transportation Statistics. *Pocket Guide to Transportation, 2006*. Washington, DC: U.S. Department of Transportation.

[6] Bureau of Transportation Statistics. *Pocket Guide to Transportation, 2007*.

[7] Greg Schneider. "Terror Risk Cited for Cargo Carried on Passenger Jets; 2 Reports List Security Gaps." *The Washington Post*, June 10, 2002.

[8] "House To Consider Bill Today Requiring Additional Cargo Screening," *Transportation Weekly*, January 9, 2007, p. 7.
[9] "The World's Top 50 Cargo Airlines," *Air Cargo World*, September 2006, pp. 22-26.
[10] Michael Fabey. "Cargo's Security Scare." *Traffic World*, December 17, 2007, p. 29.
[11] United Kingdom Air Accidents Investigation Branch. *Report on the accident to Boeing 747-121, N739PA at Lockerbie, Dumfriesshire, Scotland on 21 December 1988* (Aircraft Accident Report No 2/90 (EW/C1094)), July 1990.
[12] Canadian Aviation Bureau Safety Board. Aviation Occurrence, Air India Boeing 747-237B VT-EFO, Cork, Ireland 110 Miles West, June 23, 1985.
[13] Affidavit of Assistant Special Agent in Charge, Terry D. Turchie, Before the U.S. District Court, District of Montana, April 3, 1996.
[14] National Commission on Terrorist Attacks Upon the United States. *The 9/11 Commission Report*. New York, NY: W. W. Norton & Company.
[15] Ibid.
[16] Hazardous materials or dangerous goods include explosives; gases; flammable liquids and solids; oxidizers and organic peroxides; toxic materials and infectious substances; radioactive materials; corrosive materials; and other miscellaneous dangerous goods (e.g. asbestos).
[17] U.S. General Accounting Office (now the Government Accountability Office, or GAO). *Aviation Safety: Undeclared Air Shipments of Dangerous Goods and DOT's Enforcement Approach*. (GAO-03-22, January 2003).
[18] National Transportation Safety Board. *Aircraft Accident Report: In-Flight Fire and Impact with Terrain, ValuJet Airlines, Flight 592, DC-9-32, N904VJ, Everglades, Near Miami, Florida, May 11, 1996* (AAR-97/06).
[19] U.S. General Accounting Office. *Aviation Safety: Undeclared Air Shipments of Dangerous Goods and DOT's Enforcement Approach*. GAO-03-22, January 2003.
[20] Federal Bureau of Investigation. "Cargo Theft's High Cost: Thieves Stealing Billions Annually." Washington, DC: July 21, 2006.
[21] U.S. General Accounting Office. *Ibid*; Department of Transportation, Office of the Inspector General. *Press Release: Six MIA Airport Employees Indicted for Stealing from Checked Passenger Bags*. December 11, 2002.
[22] FIA International Research, Ltd. *Op. cit.*
[23] Ed Badolato. "Cargo Security: High-Tech Protection, High-Tech Threats." *TR News*, 211, November-December 2000, pp. 14-17.
[24] Dave Hirschman. *Hijacked: The True Story of the Heroes of Flight 705*. (New York: William Morrow & Co, 1997).
[25] National Transportation Safety Board. Accident Brief, NTSB Identification: DCA88MA008. Available at [http://www.ntsb.gov].
[26] See 49 CFR §1544.202.
[27] Transport category airplanes include all jet-powered airplanes with 10 or more passenger seats or weighing more than 12,500 pounds maximum takeoff weight (MTOW), and all propeller-driven airplanes with 19 or more seats or weighing more than 19,000 pounds MTOW.
[28] U.S. General Accounting Office. *Post-September 11th Initiatives and Long-Term Challenges*. Statement of Gerald L. Dillingham, Testimony Before the National Commission on Terrorist Attacks Upon the United States, April 1, 2003 (GAO-03-616T); U.S. Government Accountability Office, *Aviation Security: Federal Action Needed to Strengthen Domestic Air Cargo Security*, October 2005, GAO-06-76.

Aviation Security   51

[29] An indirect air carrier refers to an entity, such as a freight forwarder, that engages indirectly in the air transportation of property on passenger aircraft (See Title 49 Code of Federal Regulations, Chapter XII, Part 1544).
[30] See S.Rept. 108-38.
[31] U.S. General Accounting Office. *Aviation Security.*
[32] U.S. Department of Homeland Security, Transportation Security Administration. *Air Cargo Strategic Plan.* November 13, 2003; Department of Homeland Security, Transportation Security Administration, "Air Cargo Security Requirements, Final Rule," *Federal Register, 71*(102), May 26, 2006, pp. 30477-30517; 49 CFR 1544.239.
[33] Executive Office of the President of the United States, Office of Management and Budget, *Program Assessment, Transportation Security Administration: Air Cargo Security Programs.* Washington, DC.
[34] Department of Homeland Security, Transportation Security Administration. "Air Cargo Security Requirements; Proposed Rule." *Federal Register,* (69) 217, 65258-65291.
[35] Department of Transportation, Office of the Inspector General. *Aviation Security: Federal Aviation Administration* (Report No. AV-1998-134, May 27, 1998).
[36] White House Commission on Aviation Safety and Security. *Final Report to President Clinton.* Vice President Al Gore, Chairman. February 12, 1997. Washington, DC: The White House.
[37] Ken Leiser. "Gaps in air cargo security may offer terrorism openings." *AEROTECH News and Review,* June 21, 2002, p. B2.
[38] Statement of The Honorable Kenneth M. Mead, Inspector General U.S. Department of Transportation. "Action Needed to Improve Aviation Security." Before the Committee on Governmental Affairs and the Subcommittee on Oversight of Government Management, Restructuring and the District of Columbia, United States Senate, September 25, 2001.
[39] Department Of Transportation, Office of the Inspector General. *Aviation Security: Federal Aviation Administration* (Report No. AV-1998-134, May 27, 1998).
[40] Greg Schneider. *Op. cit.*
[41] Ken Leiser, *Op. cit.*
[42] See S.Rept. 108-38. *Air Cargo Security Improvement Act: Report of the Committee on Commerce, Science, and Transportation on S. 165.* United States Senate, April 11, 2003.
[43] White House Commission on Aviation Safety and Security. *Op. cit.*
[44] See Title 49, Code of Federal Regulations, Chapter XII, Part 1544.205
[45] Bennie G. Thompson and Edward J. Markey. Letter to the Honorable David M. Walker, Comptroller General of the United States, January 29, 2008.
[46] Air Carrier Association of America, Airforwarders Association, Air Transport Association, Cargo Network Services Corporation (CNS), High Tech Shippers Coalition, International Warehouse Logistics Association, National Air Carrier Association (NACA), National Customs Brokers and Forwarders Association of America, Inc., National Fisheries Institute, Regional Airline Association, Society of American Florists, and the U.S. Chamber of Commerce, *Letter to The Honorable Daniel Inouye and The Honorable Ted Stevens,* January 8, 2007, p. 1. 47 *Ibid.*
[48] Department of Homeland Security, Office of the Press Secretary. "Aircraft Cargo Screening Program to Begin at Cincinnati/Northern Kentucky Airport." March 26, 2007; David Hughes. "Airports Conducting Air Cargo Screening Trials." *Aviation Daily,* May 7, 2007.
[49] Statement of Admiral James M. Loy, Administrator, Transportation Security Administration, Before the Senate Committee on Commerce, Science, and Transportation, On Oversight of Transportation Security, September 9, 2003.

[50] Wickens, B., "Remote Air Sampling for Canine Olfaction," *IEEE 35th International Carnahan Conference on Security Technology*, 2001, October 2001, pp. 100 - 102.
[51] P.L. 110-28, 121 Stat. 141.
[52] Matthew Yglesias, "$1.27 Trillion: The Price is Wrong," *The American* Prospect, *17*(7), July/August 2006, p. 28-32. See also, "Screening Air Cargo," *Air Safety Week*, May 9, 2005.
[53] Jeff Bliss, "Air-Cargo Screening 'A Disaster Waiting to Happen,' Critics Say," *Bloomberg.com*, November 29, 2005.
[54] Congressional Budget Office. *H.R. 1 - Implementing the 9/11 Commission Recommendations Act of 2007*, February 2, 2007.
[55] Chris Strohm, "Democrats Look To Industry To Pay for Cargo," *Government Executive Daily Briefing*, January 9, 2007.
[56] Del Quentin Weber. "Democrats, TSA Scuffle On Who Inspects Cargo." *The Washington Post*, September 8, 2007, p. D1.
[57] Ibid.
[58] "TSA Says It Will Adhere to Cargo Screening Deadlines." *World Trade, 20*(12), December 2007, p. 10.
[59] Thomas Frank, "Bill Would Order All Air Cargo Screened," *USA Today*, January 8, 2007.
[60] Air Transport Association, *ATA Issue Brief: Air Cargo Security — The Airlines View*, Washington, DC: Air Transport Association.
[61] CRS analysis of airline industry economic data presented in: Air Transport Association, *Smart Skies: A Blueprint for the Future, 2007 Economic Report*, Washington, DC: Air Transport Association.
[62] U.S. General Accounting Office. *Aviation Security*.
[63] "Northwest to drop U.S. mail; Canceled domestic routes to cost 250 ground jobs." *Detroit Free Press*, September 5, 2003.
[64] White House Commission on Aviation Safety and Security. *Op. cit.*
[65] U.S. Department of Homeland Security, Transportation Security Administration. "TSA Canine Teams Screen U.S. Mail for Explosives - Pilot Program to Expand to Airports Across the Country." Press Release 03-34, May 29, 2003.
[66] President's Commission on the United States Postal Service. *Final Recommendations of the Technology Challenges and Opportunities Subcommittee*. Washington, DC: United States Department of the Treasury [http://www.ustreas.gov/offices/domestic-finance/usps/].
[67] Department of Homeland Security, Transportation Security Administration, "Air Cargo Security Requirements, Final Rule," *Federal Register, 71*(102), May 26, 2006, pp. 30477-30517; 49 CFR 1544.239.
[68] See H.Rept. 109-699.
[69] National Public Radio. "Some Members of Congress Raising Concerns about Potential Lapses at Airports," *Morning Edition*, May 22, 2003.
[70] Henry Pierson Curtis, "Orlando Airport's Efforts Fail to Prevent Gun, Drug Smuggling." *Orlando Sentinel*, January 28, 2008.
[71] See Statement of Captain Duane Woerth, President, Air Line Pilots Association, International. *The Status of the Federal Flight Deck Officer Program*. Before the Subcommittee on Aviation, Committee on Transportation and Infrastructure, U.S. House of Representatives. Washington, DC: May 8, 2003.
[72] Federal Aviation Administration. *FAA Aerospace Forecast Fiscal Years 2003-2014*.
[73] "Electronic cargo security seals" *Frontline Solutions, 3*(6), 42 (June 2002).
[74] U.S. General Accounting Office. *Aviation Security*.

[75] David S. De Moulpied and David Waters. "Cargo Screening Techniques Become More Widely Accepted." *Port Technology International, 10,* pp. 127-129.
[76] Greg Schneider. *Op. cit.*
[77] G. Vourvopoulos and P. C. Womble. "Pulsed Fast/Thermal Neutron Analysis: A Technique for Explosives Detection." *TALANTA (54),* pp. 459-468, 2001.
[78] U.S. General Accounting Office. *Aviation Security.*
[79] National Research Council. *The Practicality of Pulsed Fast Neutron Transmission Spectroscopy for Aviation Security.* NMAB-482-6. Washington, DC: National Academy Press, 1999.
[80] National Research Council. *Assessment of the Practicality of Pulsed Fast Neutron Analysis for Aviation Security.* Washington, DC: National Academy Press, 2002.
[81] By Calvin Biesecker. "Rapiscan To Market Brijot's Stand-Off Millimeter Wave Body Scanner," *Defense Daily,* October 31, 2007.
[82] United Kingdom Air Accidents Investigation Branch. *Op. cit.*
[83] National Research Council. *Assessment of Technologies Deployed to Improve Aviation Security: First Report.* Publication NMAB-482-5. Washington, DC: National Academy Press, 1999.
[84] Ibid.
[85] Ibid.
[86] National Commission on Terrorist Attacks Upon the United States. *The 9/11 Commission Report.*
[87] U.S. Department of Homeland Security, Transportation Security Administration. *Air Cargo Strategic Plan.*
[88] Boeing Commercial Airplanes. *747-400 Airplane Characteristics for Airport Handling.* D6-58326-1, December 2002.
[89] Federal Aviation Administration, "Security Related Considerations in the Design and Operation of Transport Category Airplanes; Proposed Rule," *Federal Register,* January 5, 2007, pp. 630-639.
[90] Department of Homeland Security, Transportation Security Administration. "Air Cargo Security Requirements; Proposed Rule;" and Jeff Bliss, "Air-Cargo Screening 'A Disaster Waiting to Happen,' Critics Say," *Bloomberg.com,* November 29, 2005; Congressional Budget Office. *H.R. 1 - Implementing the 9/11 Commission Recommendations Act of 2007,* February 2, 2007.

In: Air Cargo Security
Editor: Pierre Turrión

ISBN: 978-1-62100-054-9
© 2012 Nova Science Publishers, Inc.

Chapter 2

SCREENING AND SECURING AIR CARGO: BACKGROUND AND ISSUES FOR CONGRESS[*]

Bart Elias

SUMMARY

The October 2010 discovery of two explosive devices being prepared for loading on U.S.-bound all-cargo aircraft overseas has heightened concerns over the potential use of air cargo shipments to bomb passenger and all-cargo aircraft. The incidents have renewed policy debate over air cargo security measures and have prompted some policymakers to call for comprehensive screening of all air cargo, including shipments that travel on all-cargo aircraft.

U.S. policies and strategies for protecting air cargo have focused on two main perceived threats: the bombing of a passenger airliner carrying cargo and the hijacking of a large all-cargo aircraft for use as a weapon to attack a ground target such as a major population center, critical infrastructure, or a critical national security asset.

With respect to protecting passenger airliners from explosives placed in cargo, policy debate has focused on whether risk-based targeting strategies and methods should be used to identify those shipments requiring additional scrutiny or whether all or most shipments should be subject to more intensive physical screening. While the air cargo industry and the Transportation Security Administration (TSA) have argued for

---

[*] This is an edited, reformatted and augmented version of a Congressional Research Service 7-5700 publication R41515, dated December 2, 2010.

the implementation of risk-based approaches, Congress mandated 100% screening of all cargo placed on passenger aircraft using approved methods by August 2010 (see P.L. 110-53).

While 100% of domestic air cargo now undergoes physical screening in compliance with this mandate, not all inbound international cargo shipments carried on passenger airplanes are scrutinized in this manner. TSA is working with international air cargo operators to increase the share of cargo placed on passenger flights that is screened, but 100% screening may not be achieved until August 2013. In the interim, TSA, along with Customs and Border Protection (CBP) and international partners, is relying on risk-based targeting to increase screening of air cargo, particularly shipments deemed to be high risk.

Amid renewed congressional interest on air cargo security, a number of policy issues may arise regarding

- the desirability of risk-based strategies as alternatives to 100% cargo screening and inspection;
- the adequacy of off-airport screening under the Certified Cargo Screening Program (CCSP) in conjunction with various supply chain and air cargo facility security measures;
- the costs and benefits of requiring blast resistant cargo containers to protect aircraft from in-flight explosions in cargo holds;
- the desirability of having air cargo screened by employees of private firms rather than TSA and CBP employees; and
- cooperative efforts with international partners and stakeholders to improve the security of international air cargo operations.

THE AIR CARGO INDUSTRY

The air cargo industry consists of a complex distribution network linking manufacturers and shippers to freight forwarders, off-airport freight consolidators, and airport sorting and cargo handling facilities where shipments are loaded and unloaded from aircraft.[1] Cargo placed on aircraft travels both domestically and internationally and is widely regarded as a vital component of U.S. trade and commerce. While only a small fraction of cargo shipments travels by air, items shipped on aircraft generally consist of time-sensitive and high-value commodities. By weight, air freight comprised only 0.4% of all commercial freight activity in the United States, but accounted for 25.1% of the value of commodities shipped as freight in 2007.[2]

Common examples of air cargo include high-value machine parts and manufacturing equipment, electronic components for manufactured goods, consumer electronics, jewelry, and perishable items such as flowers, fruits, and fresh fish. Specialized freight that requires specific handling— such as unique scientific instruments, highly specialized tools and equipment, and even thoroughbred horses—is also transported as air cargo. Most outbound air cargo packages are consolidated at off-airport facilities and arrive at airports on bulk pallets or in special containers known as unit load devices. It is estimated that about 75% of all air cargo travels on bulk pallets.[3]

Typically, shippers have no foreknowledge of the particular route or aircraft by which a package will be transported. Freight forwarders and airlines make such determinations, using logistics software, databases, and computerized flight schedules to optimize the flow of air cargo. Both domestic and international air cargo movements generally rely on a hub-and-spoke network of airports to link origins and destinations. Most international air cargo that enters the United States transits through large hub facilities in Europe and Asia.

Business and consumer demand for the fast and efficient shipment of goods has fueled rapid growth in the air cargo industry over the past 30 years. Although sluggish economic growth has had the effect of reducing air cargo shipments considerably over the past two years, the Federal Aviation Administration (FAA) forecasts a return to annual growth rates in air cargo movements of about 1.3% domestically and 4.7% on international routes over the next 10 years.[4] According to Boeing Commercial Airplanes, worldwide air cargo traffic has rebounded in 2010 and is forecast to triple over the next 20 years, with 5.9% annual growth anticipated.[5]

Slightly more than 19 billion pounds of cargo were shipped on domestic flights in 2009. Of this, FedEx transported more than 10 billion pounds, while rival UPS carried more than 5.5 billion pounds. Collectively, these two carriers transported about 83% of all domestic air cargo in 2009, and were by far the largest two operators in the U.S. air cargo industry.

Additionally, in 2009, approximately 15.7 billion pounds of international air cargo were transported to and from the United States. While FedEx and UPS were the largest carriers by volume, combined they transported only about 15% of international air cargo to and from the United States. Their comparatively smaller role in the international sector reflects a greater number and diversity of air carriers that transport cargo that originates overseas.

Passenger aircraft play a much greater role in transporting air cargo internationally than within the United States. On international routes, roughly one-third of air cargo by weight is transported on passenger aircraft, compared to only 7% in domestic markets.[6] This characteristic is of particular interest with respect to potential security vulnerabilities, as cargo shipments could provide a means of placing explosive devices aboard international passenger flights destined for the United States.

SECURITY THREATS TO AIR CARGO

Despite concern over the potential use of air cargo to introduce an explosive device aboard a passenger aircraft, no such attack has ever occurred. The concern is largely predicated on the belief that more stringent measures to screen passengers and baggage may cause terrorists to consider that explosive devices in air cargo are less likely to be detected. In 1994, after a plot to place bombs in passenger cabins aboard multiple trans-Pacific flights—the so-called "Bojinka plot"—unraveled following a fire at a terrorist bomb-making site in the Philippines, Ramzi Yousef and Khalid Sheikh Mohammed allegedly pursued a plot to bomb U.S.-bound cargo planes.[7] In February 2005, Yousef was arrested in Pakistan before the plot was carried out.

The air cargo system is not particularly suitable for terrorists seeking to bomb a specific flight or even to generate attention by bombing a passenger flight, as shippers typically lack control or foreknowledge of how or when a shipment will travel. Reflecting this thinking, TSA's air cargo security strategy focuses on two primary security threats: (1) the introduction of an explosive device on a passenger aircraft, and (2) the hijacking of an all-cargo aircraft in order to use it as a weapon of mass destruction.[8]

The potential use of a hijacked all-cargo aircraft as a weapon of mass destruction was illustrated in a dramatic incident that occurred on April 7, 1994, several years prior to the 9/11 attacks. In that incident, an off-duty Federal Express flight engineer attempted to hijack a FedEx DC-10 aircraft and crash it into the company's Memphis, TN, headquarters. The hijacker boarded the airplane in Memphis under the guise of seeking free transportation (a practice known in the industry as deadheading) to San Jose, CA. His only luggage was a guitar case that concealed hammers, mallets, a knife, and a spear gun. At the time, there was no federal requirement or company procedure to screen personnel or personal baggage carried aboard cargo aircraft. The three flight crew members thwarted the hijacker's attempt to take over the airplane and made a successful emergency landing in Memphis despite sustaining serious injuries.[9]

While TSA strategies for all-cargo operations have focused most intensely on the hijacking threat, recent events suggest that terrorists may again be seeking to target U.S.-bound air cargo shipments by exploiting weaknesses in air cargo security overseas. On October 29, 2010, intelligence and law enforcement agencies in Dubai, United Arab Emirates, and in the United Kingdom discovered explosive devices concealed in packages shipped as air cargo bound for the United States. According to media reports, the explosives were not detected by initial screening, but were discovered upon reexamination after authorities received a tipoff from a member of the al Qaeda terrorist organization who had turned himself over to officials in Saudi Arabia prior to the incident. One of the devices had traveled on two passenger flights, from Yemen to Qatar and then from Qatar to Dubai, before being prepared for loading on a U.S-bound all-cargo aircraft.[10] Authorities in the United Kingdom surmised that the explosives, concealed in printer cartridges, were probably intended to detonate in flight and were capable of bringing down the aircraft.[11]

The devices originated in Yemen and are believed to be the work of al Qaeda in the Arabian Peninsula, a terrorist group that is also believed to have been responsible for the attempted bombing of a Detroit-bound passenger airliner on December 25, 2009. The group has also claimed responsibility for the crash of a UPS cargo airplane near Dubai on September 3, 2010, although the initial investigation of that crash did not uncover any evidence of a bomb.[12] The devices found in the October incidents and used in the December 2009 attempt contained pentaerythiritol tetranitrate (PETN), a powerful explosive, in quantities considered sufficient by explosives experts to cause catastrophic damage to a large airliner if detonated during flight.[13]

Following the discovery of these explosive devices shipped as air cargo, the United States temporarily suspended air cargo shipments from Yemen, and has indicated that it will work closely with Yemeni authorities to improve their cargo screening procedures and security measures.[14] Some European countries have taken additional steps to prohibit cargo shipments from Somalia as well as the carriage of large printer cartridges in the cabins of passenger aircraft. Also, Germany took further action suspending all inbound passenger flights from Yemen soon after the incident.[15] A week after the incident, the United States prohibited cargo shipments from Somalia as well. TSA also banned the shipment of printer cartridges weighing more than one pound in cargo or checked baggage, and implemented additional screening requirements for cargo deemed to be high risk.[16] Following an unrelated incident in early November 2010 involving three packages containing explosives that were addressed to European heads of state, Greece temporarily suspended all outbound international parcel shipments by air and airmail.[17]

The discovery of the explosives shipped from Yemen apparently intended to detonate in flight aboard all-cargo aircraft may require a rethinking of the generally accepted belief that bombing an all-cargo aircraft is less attractive to terrorists than bombing a passenger plane. Much remains unknown about the motives and objectives behind these incidents. The possibility that the terrorists intended to bring about more restrictive regulations and thus cause widespread economic damage to the air cargo industry cannot be excluded.[18]

Regardless of motive, the policy response to these incidents has raised anew the debate between advocates of a risk-based strategy that relies heavily on characteristics of a shipment to identify packages for increased scrutiny and supporters of approaches in which all or most shipments are subject to some form of physical inspection. Proponents of comprehensive physical screening argue that it is the only way to ensure adequate security, while advocates of risk-based approaches argue that comprehensive screening is too costly, too time consuming, and given the current state of technology, potentially no better than well designed targeting strategies. At present, the United States requires more extensive physical screening for shipments placed on passenger aircraft than for shipments aboard cargo planes, in accordance with a statutory mandate for 100% screening of all such cargo. However, TSA has stated it may not reach fully compliance with the mandate to screen all cargo aboard inbound international passenger flights until August 2013.[19]

CURRENT LEGISLATIVE ISSUES

Following the October 2010 discovery of explosives in cargo originating in Yemen, there has been renewed interest in requiring that all air cargo, not just that placed on passenger aircraft, be subject to physical screening. On November 16, 2010, Representative Markey introduced the Air Cargo Security Act (H.R. 6410, 111th Congress), to require screening of all cargo transported on all-cargo aircraft, including U.S.-bound international shipments, in a manner commensurate with the screening requirements for passenger checked baggage. The legislation also includes provisions requiring inspections of foreign air cargo shipping facilities that handle U.S.-bound flights and formal security training programs for cargo handlers. On November 17, 2010, Senator Casey introduced a similar measure (S. 3954, 111th Congress) in the Senate.

POTENTIAL CHALLENGES FOR ALL-CARGO SCREENING

TSA lacks the direct authority to define screening requirements at foreign airports for U.S.-bound cargo. TSA could impose regulations on foreign carriers, as well as U.S. carriers, stipulating minimum air cargo security standards and requirements, including 100% screening using certain approved methods. However, enforcement overseas would be up to authorities in other countries. If they do not concur with the U.S. approach, disagreement over security standards could complicate U.S. foreign relations and could potentially impact foreign trade.

The impact of 100% screening on the air cargo industry could be considerable as associated costs may be difficult to fully pass on to shipping costumers. The Congressional Budget Office estimated a cost of $250 million in the first year and $650 million per year for the following five years, for a total of $3.5 billion over six years, to implement the mandate for 100% baggage screening on passenger aircraft.[20] Previous CRS estimates concluded that the cost may be somewhat lower, totaling about $3.75 billion over the first 10 years of implementation.[21] However, more recent estimates suggest that industry-wide compliance with the 100% screening mandate may cost more than $700 million in the first year.[22]

Given that these estimates cover only shipments placed on passenger aircraft, which make up about 10% of all cargo shipped to and within the United States by air, the projected cost of physically screening all air cargo could conceivably total several billion dollars annually. The logistical challenges of screening all air cargo may also be significant, as demonstrated by the complexities of meeting the 100% screening mandate for cargo aboard domestic passenger flights and the continuing difficulties in screening all inbound international cargo placed on passenger flights. In addition, there is potential for full physical screening of all air cargo to lead to shipping delays and other inefficiencies.

With respect to the federal budget, air cargo may become an issue of increasing focus following the October 2010 explosives incidents. The President's request for FY2011 sought a slight decrease in funding for air cargo security measures, seeking $118 million compared to $123 million appropriated in FY2010. The Senate-reported FY2011 appropriations bill (S. 3607, 111th Congress) specified $122 million, with the additional funds above the requested level to accelerate hiring of additional inspectors and expanding canine cooperative programs with state and local law enforcement in order to support current cargo screening mandates.[23] This funding increase has not been enacted.

INTERNATIONAL COOPERATION

With regard to all-cargo operations, there is no statutory or regulatory requirement for screening, and according to industry estimates, the overall percentage of international shipments screened prior to transit to the United States may be as low as 50%.[24] TSA concedes that screening international cargo poses unique challenges and constraints due to shippers' limited control over their foreign supply chains, the scale and diversity of worldwide supply chains, and diplomatic considerations.[25]

To address theses challenges, TSA's International Air Cargo Workgroup has developed a risk-based rating system and scheduling tool to prioritize air cargo facility inspections overseas. In 2008, the TSA entered into a bilateral agreement with the European Union as well as a quadrilateral agreement on air cargo security with the European Union, Canada, and Australia.[26] More broadly, it is working closely with the International Civil Aviation Organization (ICAO) to draft worldwide standards for all-cargo security, which will probably entail a lengthy period of implementation.[27]

TSA has 10 international cargo transportation security inspectors deployed to field offices in Los Angeles, Dallas-Fort Worth, Miami, and Frankfurt, Germany. The role of these inspectors is to examine cargo operations at the last points of departure to the United States and assess compliance with screening and security requirements. Additionally, TSA has eight international industrial representatives who work with about 240 foreign passenger and all-cargo air carriers that operate flights to the United States. These individuals have responsibility for ensuring foreign air carrier compliance with TSA regulations, including those pertaining to the screening and security of air cargo.[28] Given the volume of international air cargo, the potential threat posed by international shipments, and the extensive reliance on passenger aircraft to haul cargo from overseas, the size of the TSA's international inspector and industrial representative workforce may be an area of particular interest to Congress.

RISK-BASED EVALUATIONS OF SHIPMENTS

Under the current air cargo security system, a number of risk-based strategies are being employed to evaluate the security risk of air cargo shipments.

The Known Shipper Program

The principal means for pre-screening or profiling cargo has been through the use of air carrier and freight forwarder "known shipper" programs. In May 2006, TSA issued a final rule database may not be placed aboard passenger aircraft, even if they are screened or inspected physically. This applies to inbound international flights as well as domestic flights.

Before the industry-wide KSDB was created, some air carriers and freight forwarders had voluntarily participated in a system using a central database of known shippers to vet cargo destined for passenger aircraft as required under the Aviation and Transportation Security Act of 2001 (ATSA, P.L. 107-71). Other air carriers and freight forwarders relied on internal databases and security protocols approved by TSA for determining whether shipments bound for a passenger airplane originated from known sources applying approved security measures to protect the integrity of those shipments.

The development of known shipper programs in the mid-1990s was prompted by industry experts and Congress. Key concerns included the need for increased compliance with guidelines for the shipment of hazardous materials and the need to deter terrorists from using cargo as a means to place explosives or incendiary devices on aircraft. In addition, congressional hearings regarding the 1996 Valujet crash in Miami that resulted from a cargo hold fire concluded that air cargo safety could be achieved only through a comprehensive inspection program encompassing all components of the air cargo network.[31]

In December 1996, FAA's Aviation Security Advisory Committee Security Baseline Working Group issued a series of recommendations that formed the basis for FAA's effort to strengthen air cargo safety and security. The White House Commission on Aviation Safety and Security, formed after the 1996 crash of TWA Flight 800 and commonly referred to as the Gore Commission, urged adoption of the recommendations of the Baseline Working Group regarding the profiling of "known" and "unknown" shippers.[32] FAA subsequently established a known shipper program, outlining procedures for freight forwarders and air carriers to review the security practices of known frequent customers and establish a cargo security plan for handling cargo from known and unknown shippers. With the passage of ATSA in 2001, oversight of cargo security measures was transferred from FAA to TSA. TSA has continued to rely on known shipper programs as a principal means for pre-screening air cargo.

A central issue regarding the post-9/11 implementation of known shipper programs was the creation of a consolidated database. TSA initially instituted a voluntary industry-wide database. This initiative poised TSA to address congressional interest in establishing a mandatory industrywide known shipper database, as urged by the Senate during the 108th Congress (see S. 165, S. 2845 as passed by the Senate). The administration's subsequent regulatory action to require an industry-wide known shipper database led Congress to ultimately drop a Senate-passed statutory requirement from the Intelligence Reform Act of 2004 (P.L. 108-458). Congress instead settled on language directing TSA to issue final rules on air cargo security, including an industry-wide known shipper database, by September 2005. The final rules were announced in May 2006.

Vulnerability Assessments and Risk-Based Targeting

Reflecting concerns over the logistics and costs associated with mandatory cargo screening, air cargo industry stakeholders have voiced considerable opposition to requiring 100% screening of passenger air cargo, urging Congress instead to "focus on realistic solutions based on a framework that identifies and prioritizes risks, works methodically to apply effective and practical security programs, and makes optimal use of federal and industry resources."[33] The industry has continually advocated for a risk-based screening system that incorporates threat assessment and targeting capabilities, provides incentives for shippers to strengthen supply chain measures, and focuses increased inspections on cargo determined to be of elevated risk through risk assessment and targeting capabilities.

These arguments roughly parallel TSA's former strategic plan for air cargo security, which, prior to congressional mandates for 100% screening of cargo placed on passenger aircraft, focused on risk-based targeted screening of cargo. The industry specifically recommended increased use of canine explosives detection teams; enhanced supply chain security; enhanced targeting of shipments based on CBP experience with the Automated

Targeting System (ATS); expanded use of explosive trace detection technology for targeted screening; and accelerated research and development of technologies that can more efficiently inspect elevated-risk cargo.[34]

While all domestic air cargo placed on passenger airplanes now undergoes physical screening, TSA employs random and risk-based assessments of inbound international shipments or domestic shipments carried on all-cargo aircraft. In these cases, it uses a combination of risk-based targeting strategies and vulnerability assessments of airports and operators to focus screening efforts on suspicious "high risk" cargo. TSA is continuing to work with international partners to apply risk-based strategies until 100% screening of cargo placed on inbound international passenger flights can be achieved. Additionally, TSA and CBP have jointly developed a risk assessment process using CBP's ATS and TSA's vulnerability assessment methodology.[35]

Under CBP's "advance manifest rule," carriers operating inbound international flights must forward cargo manifest information to CBP four hours prior to arrival in the United States. The four-hour requirement is relevant in carrying out CBP's mission of screening items as they enter the United States, but may be inadequate for use in targeting shipments from an aviation security standpoint. In many cases, aircraft may have departed for the United States before CBP receives the manifest information and analyzes it using ATS to identify high risk cargo. This concern does not apply to flights originating in Canada, Mexico, and the Caribbean, for which CBP requires the manifest information before wheels up.

Whereas CBP's mission is focused on detecting threats to the United States arriving at points of entry, including U.S. airports, TSA's aviation security mission considers threats to airborne aircraft before they enter U.S. airspace. A considerable policy question arising from the October 2010 incidents is the adequacy of current manifest screening requirements and targeting procedures for detecting potential threats to U.S.-bound flights. Congress may want to gain a better understanding of whether earlier transmittal of manifest information could improve targeting capabilities aimed at identifying high risk cargo and, if so, what potential impacts such requirements may have on international air cargo shipments.

Prior to the October 2010 incidents in which explosives were discovered in U.S.-bound air cargo shipments, efforts to expand risk-based targeting of shipments in the all-cargo sector had reportedly languished over concerns regarding potential operational impacts. For example, the *Wall Street Journal* reported that efforts to develop more sophisticated risk profiles for vetting overnight packages had apparently stalled over concerns that thresholds for inspections may be set too low, causing potential delays in the delivery of time-sensitive shipments.[36]

Following the October 2010 incidents, TSA applied additional screening measures to inbound international air cargo assessed to be high risk.[37] While the specific details of how TSA assesses risk are regarded as sensitive security information, factors may include country of origin and possibly risk scores based on data regarding the sender, the recipient, and other characteristics of the shipment. For example, cash payment of shipping costs may be considered an indicator of risk in certain markets, although this characteristic, by itself, may not raise suspicion in all cases.

CARGO SCREENING PROCEDURES

Whereas the air cargo industry has favored risk-based approaches for both cargo planes and cargo aboard passenger aircraft, some policymakers have argued that more comprehensive screening of cargo is needed to make cargo security comparable to that of passengers and baggage. Congress responded to these arguments in a series of enactments since the 9/11 terrorist attacks.

The first of these laws, ATSA, established a requirement for screening and inspection of all individuals, goods, property, vehicles, and other equipment entering a secured area of a passenger airport. The law mandated that other areas of airports have the same level of protection as passenger terminals, but did not require the use of any specific screening technologies or techniques.

ATSA required TSA to provide for the screening of cargo placed on passenger aircraft, but did not specify how such screening was to be carried out. ATSA also directed that a system to screen, inspect, or otherwise ensure the security of all-cargo aircraft be established as soon as practicable, but set no specific deadlines. Additionally, aircraft operators were required to establish controls over cargo shipments to prevent the carriage of unauthorized explosive or incendiary devices aboard passenger aircraft and access by unauthorized individuals.

The Homeland Security Appropriations Act of 2005 (P.L. 108-334) called for tripling the proportion of cargo on passenger airplanes that is screened or inspected. FY2006 appropriations language (P.L. 109-90) directed TSA to take all possible measures—including the certification, procurement, and deployment of screening systems—to inspect and screen air cargo on passenger aircraft and increase the percentage of cargo inspected beyond the level mandated in the FY2005 appropriations measure. A year later, FY2007 appropriations language (P.L. 109-295) directed TSA to work with industry stakeholders to develop standards and protocols to increase the use of explosives detection equipment for screening air cargo. Similarly, the FY2008 Omnibus Appropriations Act (P.L. 110-161) directed the parent agency of both TSA and CBP, the Department of Homeland Security (DHS), to research, develop, and procure new technologies to screen air cargo, and, in the interim, to utilize checked baggage explosives detection equipment to the maximum extent practicable to screen air cargo placed on passenger aircraft.

The Implementing the 9/11 Commission Recommendations Act of 2007 (P.L. 110-53), enacted in August 2007, required 100% physical screening and inspection of all cargo placed on passenger aircraft by August 2010, with an interim requirement to screen 50% of such cargo by February 2009. The act specified screening methods acceptable in meeting this requirement, including X-ray systems, explosives detection systems, explosives trace detection, TSA-certified explosives detection canine teams, and physical searches conducted in conjunction with manifest verifications. Additional methods may be approved by TSA. However, the act specifies that cargo documents and known shipper verification, by themselves, are not acceptable screening methods.

The act, however, did not specify who is to conduct the screening. TSA has interpreted the language to allow airlines, freight forwarders, or, in some cases, shippers, manufacturers, and third party screening facilities to conduct screening at off-airport locations, so long as they can assure the security of a shipment until it is loaded onto an aircraft.[38] TSA maintains that this is the only viable means for meeting the mandate for 100% physical screening, as it lacks the resources to screen the volume of cargo placed on passenger aircraft using TSA employees.[39] TSA's approach, implemented through its voluntary Certified Cargo Screening Program (CCSP), has pushed much of the operational cost associated with cargo screening and inspection on to the airlines, freight forwarders, and shippers. The extent to which air carriers and freight forwarders have been able to pass along these costs to shippers and consumers may be an issue of particular interest to Congress.

Mandatory screening requirements for cargo on passenger flights may place passenger airlines at a competitive disadvantage against all-cargo airlines, so long as all-cargo carriers face less stringent requirements. In addition, if security screening requirements discourage shipments on passenger flights, some routes may no longer be profitable for airlines.[40] Given that most large passenger airlines have failed to achieve consistent profitability in recent years, the direct and indirect costs associated with a mandate to screen all cargo may present particular financial challenges to the airlines.

While estimated cargo revenues of about $4.7 billion[41] annually make up only about 5% of total industry-wide operating revenues among U.S. passenger air carriers, these additional revenues can make the difference between profit or loss for passenger airlines.[42]

Beyond the economic impact, the prospect of screening 100% of air cargo placed on passenger aircraft has raised a number of challenges due to a lack of suitable bulk screening technologies. TSA and industry experts concluded that the only viable means of meeting the August 2010 deadline was to conduct screening at the piece level at various points in the supply chain and then to impose a variety of measures to secure cargo after screening it at off-airport locations. In order to address these complexities, TSA established the voluntary CCSP, allowing shippers, manufacturers, warehouses, and off-airport cargo consolidation facilities to screen cargo destined for passenger aircraft.

The Certified Cargo Screening Program (CCSP)

Screening pallets and containers can be complex, potentially requiring that the shipments be broken down so that individual items can be examined. CCSP is intended to minimize these logistical complexities by allowing screening to occur at factories, warehouses, third party logistics providers, and off-airport cargo consolidation facilities, so long as the operator of the facility tenders cargo to either an air carrier or a freight forwarder.[43] TSA must approve the screening procedures as well as supply chain security measures to prevent tampering with shipments once they have been screened, and it audits participants' performance. The CCSP program is voluntary, but widespread industry participation reflects considerable perceived benefits.[44]

To participate in CCSP, employers must allow TSA to conduct security threat assessments to check the names of workers with access to air cargo against government terrorist watchlists. The cost of doing so, currently a one-time fee of $19 per worker, is fully recovered from fees charged to CCSP participants. In FY2011, TSA anticipates collecting $5.2 million in fees to vet almost 275,000 cargo handlers and other supply-chain employees covered under CCSP. This is in addition to about 200,000 employees at CCSP facilities that completed security threat assessments in FY2010. By late August 2010, just after the 100% screening mandate went into effect, over 1,000 facilities—including more than 500 indirect air carrier facilities, almost 100 independent cargo screening facilities, and almost 400 shippers—had been certified under the CCSP program. As these totals represent only a fraction of the domestic air cargo industry, considerable expansion of the program is anticipated during FY2011.

CARGO SCREENING TECHNOLOGIES

TSA reported in August 2010 that 100% of cargo placed on domestic passenger flights undergoes approved physical screening in compliance with statutory requirements set forth in the Implementing Recommendations of the 9/11 Commission Act of 2007 (P.L. 110-53).[45] However, TSA recently indicated that 100% screening of all inbound international air cargo transported on passenger aircraft may not be achieved until August 2013.[46]

TSA has approved a number of x-ray, bulk explosives detection systems and explosives trace detection machines for screening air cargo to meet the requirements of the screening mandate.[47] Essentially, these are adaptations of technologies used extensively for screening checked baggage and carry-on items. However, none of these devices is approved for the screening of palletized or containerized cargo. Procedures stipulate that screening must instead be done on individual cargo items since available technologies, especially explosives detection systems, impose considerable limits on the size of the object that can be screened. Currently available systems can only accommodate objects slightly more than 3 feet wide and about 8 feet long, far too small for large cargo items, much less cargo containers and pallets. The limitations of explosives detection systems in the air cargo environment have led to extensive reliance on explosives trace detection, particularly at airport screening locations, coupled with canine teams.

TSA has trained over 500 law enforcement canine teams at 78 airports. Under cooperative agreements, TSA pays for the training, certification, and maintenance of the dogs and partially reimburses law enforcement agencies for handler salaries and other costs. These teams devote about 25% of their time to air cargo screening. In addition, TSA has about 150 of its own canine teams that screen cargo at the 20 busiest airports in terms of cargo shipments aboard passenger planes. These teams focus on screening large bulk cargo configurations that cannot be efficiently screened using currently available technologies.[48]

In FY2010, TSA carried out a pilot program at 18 locations to evaluate the effectiveness of selected screening technologies and chain-of-custody procedures.[49] Participating facilities were reimbursed up to $375,000 each for acquisition of a mix of security screening technologies. In exchange, these sites were required to provide TSA with detailed reports of cargo volumes and the effectiveness and efficiency of screening technologies used. The study concluded in August 2010. TSA is now assessing the performance of the various screening technologies and methods employed. To date, however, the only approved technologies for cargo screening require examination of individual items. It is estimated that palletized cargo makes up 75% of all cargo carried on passenger planes.[50] The lack of an approved technology for screening pallets leaves the industry dependent on work-around solutions, largely involving the off-airport screening of cargo coupled with approved supply-chain security measures to prevent tampering after the item is screened under CCSP procedures.

Imaging systems are employed at seaports and border crossings to scrutinize entire trucks and multimodal containers. These systems, which use a variety of gamma-ray, x-ray, x-ray backscatter, and millimeter wave imaging technologies, are generally not considered suitable in the air cargo domain because they require intensive human observation to detect potential threats. They generally do not offer adequate image resolution or automated or assisted threat detection capabilities for identifying relatively small explosive devices capable of destroying an airliner.

Neutron beam technologies offer a potential solution, allowing automated explosives detection capabilities of containerized and palletized cargo. Under a pilot program, a pulsed fast neutron analysis scanner was installed at Houston's George Bush Intercontinental Airport in 2005, at a cost of $8 million. The unit was touted as a potential means to automatically screen large containers and bulk cargo shipments for explosives as well as for hazardous chemicals, radiological and nuclear materials, and other potential threats based on sub-atomic properties. In 2007, the pilot program was suspended, reportedly for financial reasons, despite high detection rates and low false alarm rates across a wide range of threat types and container sizes.[51] The technology is being used to screen cargo and baggage in Singapore and Hong Kong, and to screen truck containers at a border checkpoint in El Paso, TX.[52] However, the high cost and large footprint of the machines have been significant deterrents to their use in the air cargo industry.

Absent a suitable technology for screening palletized and containerized cargo at airport facilities, the reliance on off-airport cargo screening under CCSP and the logistic demands of the air cargo industry pose unique challenges for maintaining security throughout the supply chain.

SUPPLY CHAIN SECURITY MEASURES

A variety of supply chain security measures provides options for preventing and detecting tampering and maintaining the integrity of cargo shipments. These measures include tamper-evident and tamper-resistant packaging, cargo tracking technologies, and identifiers to designate screened cargo.

Tamper-Evident and Tamper-Resistant Packaging

Various technologies exist for sealing cargo shipments and cargo containers to prevent tampering. Relatively low cost solutions such as tamper-evident tapes that provide visual indications of tampering are readily available and could easily be implemented during packaging. Such technology could be used in combination with "known shipper" protocols to insure that known shippers provide sufficient security in their packaging facilities and to deter tampering and theft during shipping and handling. Tamper-evident tape may also be an effective tool to deter cargo theft and the introduction of contraband, counterfeit, and pirated goods during shipment.

At cargo handling facilities, tamper-evident seals and locks can be utilized on cargo containers to prevent theft and the introduction of contraband or threat objects. Electronic seals may serve as an additional deterrent by providing more immediate detection of tampering. Electronic seals have alarms, some triggered by fiber optic cable loops, that transmit a signal when tampered with.[53]

Electronic seals cost about $2,500 per unit, but are reusable. However, currently available seals have a limited transmission range, which may make it difficult to detect tampering. In addition, there is concern that the signals may interfere with aircraft electronic systems.[54]

Tracking Technologies

The air cargo industry, particularly the express package sector, relies on tracking technologies such as global positioning systems and radio-frequency identification to process, sort, and track shipments. The technology also has potential security applications. Tracking technologies could identify suspicious origins or unexplained delays or detours in transit.

Screened Cargo Identifiers

TSA relies primarily on a system of identifiers to designate that a piece of cargo has been properly screened and is eligible for shipment on passenger aircraft. TSA approves a variety of stickers, stamps, and tags to be used as screened cargo identifiers.[55] The security and integrity of these identifiers is a key element of CCSP, as stolen or counterfeit identifiers could be used to pass off unscreened cargo as screened. Measures to account for all identifiers appear to be vital components of supply chain security. However, given the highly diverse and geographically distributed nature of the supply chain, it may be difficult to detect falsified or counterfeit stamps beyond the point of screening. The effectiveness of CCSP in maintaining package integrity beyond the point of screening may be an issue of particular interest to Congress.

SECURITY OF AIR CARGO FACILITIES AND OPERATIONS

Air cargo operators and freight forwarders in the United States and at overseas locations that handle U.S.-bound shipments must apply TSA-approved security programs. TSA has not publicly released the specific requirements of these programs. Broadly, these programs include access control measures, site surveillance and physical security, mandatory background checks and security threat assessments of air cargo workers, and employee security training and awareness.

- Major passenger airlines must implement TSA's Aircraft Operator Standard Security Program, including detailed security measures for transported cargo.
- All-cargo operators that operate any aircraft weighing roughly 100,000 pounds (45,000 kg) or more, such as FedEx, UPS, and operators of large freight aircraft, are covered under the Full All-Cargo Aircraft Operator Standard Security Program.
- Cargo operators and charter operators that also consign cargo shipments aboard aircraft that are larger than 12,500 pounds but less than roughly 100,000 pounds must implement a TSA-approved Twelve-Five Standard Security Program.
- Domestic freight forwarders must implement an Indirect Air Carrier Standard Security Program (IACSSP).

- Other components of the air cargo network, such as shippers, third party logistics companies, and independent air cargo consolidation and screening facilities, may voluntarily participate in the CCSP.

IN-FLIGHT SECURITY MEASURES

In-flight air cargo security options address the primary perceived vulnerabilities of a potential hijacking of an all-cargo flight or the bombing of a passenger aircraft using an explosive device carried in a cargo shipment. Protecting access to the cockpit and arming all-cargo pilots have been viewed as the primary in-flight options to reduce the vulnerability of all-cargo aircraft to potential hijackings. Blast-resistant cargo containers are being considered as an option to protect passenger airliners from explosives.

Hardened Cockpit Doors and Protective Barriers

While ATSA required the installation of hardened cockpit doors, FAA regulations exempted all-cargo aircraft from the requirement after the FY2003 appropriations act (see P.L. 108-7) limited federal funding to doors on passenger aircraft. While some cargo aircraft have hardened cockpit doors to thwart potential stowaway hijackers, many do not.

The use of protective barriers, such as metal gates and thick cable fences that are less costly than hardened cockpit doors, has been considered as a means to secure the cockpits of all-cargo aircraft. In 2007, Representative Israel introduced legislation (H.R. 3925, 110th Congress) to require installation of such barriers on all air carrier aircraft, including all-cargo aircraft. For all-cargo aircraft, the proposal left the use of the protective barrier to the pilot's discretion. The legislation won the praise of the Air Line Pilots Association (ALPA), which has advocated the installation of protective barriers on both passenger and all-cargo aircraft, but it was not adopted. In 2004, United Airlines took the initiative of installing protective barriers in addition to the required hardened cockpit doors on some of its passenger aircraft. Other airlines have not followed suit and the issue has received little attention among policymakers. A renewed focus on cargo security may revive discussion of the possible use of these barriers on all-cargo aircraft.

Arming All-Cargo Pilots

Since the 9/11 attacks the issue of arming pilots to deter hijacking and protect the cockpit in the event of hijacking attempts has been controversial, opposed by airlines and several industry experts but broadly supported by Congress. Provisions allowing pilots of passenger airliners to receive firearms training and fly armed were included in the Homeland Security Act of 2002 (P.L. 107-296). The act, however, did not allow for all-cargo pilots to participate in the program, despite concern about the risk of hijackings by stowaways.

During the 108th Congress, proponents of arming all-cargo pilots urged Congress to allow all-cargo pilots to join the ranks of passenger airline pilots who can volunteer for selection and training in the Federal Flight Deck Officers (FFDO) program. This program, established by the Homeland Security Act of 2002 (P.L. 107-296), trains and deputizes qualified pilots to carry firearms and use deadly force to protect the flight deck against terrorist attacks. While the plan was originally limited to pilots of passenger airliners, Vision 100 (P.L. 108-176) expanded the program to allow all-cargo pilots and flight engineers to participate. Air carriers, in general, have been hesitant about the program because of liability concerns, even though the Homeland Security Act extended specific liability protections to the airlines and pilot participants. Cargo airlines had opposed allowing their pilots to join the FFDO program. In any event, the program is largely limited to domestic operations due to a lack of international agreements regarding the carriage of firearms by pilots.

The FFDO program, along with other flight crew security training initiatives, has received annual appropriations of about $25 million since it was fully implemented in FY2004. Few, if any, changes to the program are expected in the near term. Nonetheless, Congress may at some point address lingering concerns such as the convenience of training and requalification sites, the carriage of firearms outside the cockpit (which is presently highly restricted), and program liability surrounding the role of the federal flight deck officer as both an airline pilot and a deputized federal officer. While the TSA has recently opened additional retraining and requalification sites in Texas and New Jersey, other aspects of the program remain unchanged.

Blast-Resistant Cargo Containers

The use of blast-resistant cargo containers has long been considered a possible option for mitigating the consequences of an in-flight explosion. The 9/11 Commission recommended the deployment of at least one hardened container on every passenger aircraft that carries cargo.[56] Stemming from this recommendation, the National Intelligence Reform Act of 2004 (P.L. 108-458) required the TSA to establish a pilot program to explore the feasibility of this concept and authorized the use of incentives to airlines to offset added fuel, maintenance, and other operational costs associated with using hardened cargo containers in an effort to encourage voluntary participation. The act authorized $2 million for the pilot program.

The Implementing the 9/11 Commission Recommendations Act of 2007 (P.L. 110-53) directed the TSA to evaluate the pilot program and, based on its findings, to implement a program to pay for, provide, and maintain blast-resistant cargo containers for use by air carriers on a risk-managed basis. However, no such program has been initiated. The airline industry and aviation experts have been skeptical of the approach because of both its direct and indirect costs, with indirect costs mostly related to additional fuel consumption and decreased payload capacity because of the additional weight of the hardened containers.

The 9/11 Commission recommended that any suspicious packages going aboard a passenger aircraft be placed in the hardened cargo container. This recommendation implies that a cargo prescreening or risk evaluation process would be used to determine what cargo should be loaded into the hardened container. A means for identifying elevated risk cargo through pre-screening would likely be needed to assess risk and determine what cargo should be placed in a hardened container. A key policy question is whether suspicious cargo should be allowed to travel on passenger aircraft even if it is secured in hardened containers. Congress may wish to debate the risks and benefits of shipping suspicious cargo in hardened containers aboard passenger airplanes compared to the alternative of offloading such shipments to all-cargo aircraft.

If only one hardened cargo container is deployed per aircraft, a relatively small fraction of available cargo space will be reinforced. For example, a Boeing 747-400 passenger jet is capable of holding up to 13 full-width, or 26 half-width containers.[57] Since one hardened container could house only a small fraction of transported air cargo, careful consideration must be given in deciding what cargo is placed inside these hardened cargo containers.

TSA INSPECTION AND OVERSIGHT OF AIR CARGO OPERATIONS

TSA is responsible for conducting regulatory compliance inspections of air carriers and freight forwarders. Additionally, manufacturers, freight consolidators, and other entities that voluntarily participate in the CCSP allow TSA to inspect and audit their security practices to ensure they meet TSA minimum standards.

TSA has regulatory oversight with regard to air cargo security matters of about 4,400 freight forwarders and about 300 air carriers.[58] Additionally, more than 1,000 facilities are participating in the CCSP. TSA has about 500 transportation security inspectors overseeing the air cargo sector.[59] While this is more than double the cargo inspector workforce in FY2006, it may still be strained by the size and complexity of the air cargo industry and the number of regulated entities. Moreover, the TSA has noted that cargo inspectors have, on occasion, participated in Visible Intermodal Prevention and Response (VIPR) teams to assist with response to elevated threat conditions. These additional duties that pull inspectors away from air cargo responsibilities could detract from TSA's ability to conduct adequate oversight of cargo security.

TSA reports that it conducts almost 3,000 random security inspections each month. Teams of TSA air cargo inspectors have also completed cargo vulnerability assessments at major cargo airports as well as assessments of other selected airports. While these accomplishments are considerable, the scope and depth of random site inspections and audits of air cargo security may be an issue of particular interest to Congress as it assesses the degree to which deficiencies in regulatory compliance are being identified and corrected.

End Notes

[1] Shippers are the owners of air cargo items and may be either individuals or businesses. Freight forwarders are brokers or middlemen that do not operate aircraft, but make arrangements for moving cargo and may operate distribution centers that store incoming shipments and then send them on to final recipients. Since freight forwarders do not operate aircraft, but provide air cargo services, they are referred to in regulation as indirect air carriers (IACs).

[2] Department of Transportation, Bureau of Transportation Statistics, *Freight Transportation: Global Highlights, 2010*, http://www.bts.gov/publications/freight_transportation/.

[3] Andy Pasztor, Keith Johnson, and Daniel Michaels, "Focus on Cargo Security Steps," *Wall Street Journal*, November 1, 2010.

[4] Federal Aviation Administration, Aviation Policy and Plans, *FAA Aerospace Forecasts, Fiscal Years 2010-2030*. Projected growth in air cargo movements is based on forecast revenue ton miles (RTMs). An RTM represents the movement of one ton of cargo a distance of one mile in revenue service.

[5] Boeing Commercial Airplanes, *World Air Cargo Forecast 2010-2011*, Seattle, WA: The Boeing World Air Cargo Forecast Team, Boeing Commercial Airplanes, http://www.boeing.com/commercial/cargo/.

[6] All statistics are based on CRS analysis of calendar year 2009 air carrier T-100 domestic and international market data reported to and maintained by the U.S. Department of Transportation, Bureau of Transportation Statistics.

[7] Mark Clayton, "Yemen Packages: Air Cargo Was a Target Before. Why Is It Still Vulnerable?," *Christian Science Monitor*, November 2, 2010.

[8] Transportation Security Administration, *Fiscal Year 2011 Congressional Justification, Aviation Security*.

[9] Dave Hirschman. *Hijacked: The True Story of the Heroes of Flight 705*. (New York: William Morrow & Co, 1997).

[10] Joseph Berger and Robert F. Worth, "Bombs Were Set to Explode Inflight; Officials in Washington Weigh Their Options for Response to Failed Attack," *International Herald Tribune*, November 1, 2010.

[11] "Air Freight from Yemen and Somalia Banned," *BBC News*, November 1, 2010.

[12] Lolita C. Baldor, "Al-Qaida Claims It Caused UPS Plane Crash in Dubai," *Washington Post*, November 5, 2010.

[13] "Cargo Bombs Were Powerful Enough to Bring Down Plane, Say Experts," *Daily Post* (Liverpool, UK), November 2, 2010.

[14] Transportation Security Administration, *Remarks As Prepared by TSA Administrator John Pistole to AVSEC World 2010*, November 2, 2010.

[15] Michael Savage and Nigel Morris, "New Restrictions Follow. Bomb Attempt," *Independent (UK)*, November 2, 2010; Tony Czuczka and Patrick Donahue, "Germany Bans Yemen Flights, Considers Further Security Measures," *Bloomberg Businessweek*, November 4, 2010.

[16] Derek Kravitz and Ashley Halsey III, "U.S. Tightening Air Cargo Security," *Washington Post*, November 9, 2010.

[17] "Greece Halts Air Cargo after Bombs Target European Leaders," *Voice of America VOA News*, November 3, 2010; "Greece Suspends International Parcels After Further Explosive Devices Found," *CEP-Research*, November 3, 2010.

[18] Robert W. Poole, Jr., "Fighting the Last War on Air Cargo," *Airport Policy News*, Issue 62, November 2010, Los Angeles, CA: The Reason Foundation.

[19] Thomas Frank, Alan Levin, and Kevin Johnson, "Bomb Plot Shows Gaps in Screening of Air Cargo," *USA Today*, November 1, 2010.

[20] Congressional Budget Office, *H.R. 1 - Implementing the 9/11 Commission Recommendations Act of 2007*, February 2, 2007.

[21] See CRS Report RL34390, *Aviation Security: Background and Policy Options for Screening and Securing Air Cargo*, by Bart Elias.

[22] Katie Johnston Chase, "Push On for Cargo Screening," *Boston Globe*, November 2, 2010.

[23] See CRS Report R41189, *Homeland Security Department: FY2011 Appropriations*, coordinated by Chad C. Haddal.

[24] Andy Pasztor, Keith Johnson, and Daniel Michaels, "Focus on Cargo Security Steps," *Wall Street Journal*, November 1, 2010.

[25] Transportation Security Administration, *Fiscal Year 2011 Congressional Justification, Aviation Security.*
[26] Transportation Security Administration. *Programs and Initiatives: Air Cargo,* http://www.tsa.gov/what_we_do/tsnm/air_cargo/programs.shtm.
[27] Transportation Security Administration, *Fiscal Year 2011 Congressional Justification, Aviation Security.*
[28] Transportation Security Administration, *Fiscal Year 2011 Congressional Justification, Aviation Security.*
[29] Department of Homeland Security, Transportation Security Administration. "Air Cargo Security Requirements; Proposed Rule." *Federal Register,* (69) 217, 65258-65291.
[30] Transportation Security Administration, *Air Cargo, Transportation Sector Network Management.*
[31] Department of Transportation, Office of the Inspector General. *Aviation Security: Federal Aviation Administration* (Report No. AV-1998-134, May 27, 1998).
[32] White House Commission on Aviation Safety and Security. *Final Report to President Clinton.* Vice President Al Gore, Chairman. February 12, 1997. Washington, DC: The White House.
[33] Air Carrier Association of America, Airforwarders Association, Air Transport Association, Cargo Network Services Corporation (CNS), High Tech Shippers Coalition, International Warehouse Logistics Association, National Air Carrier Association (NACA), National Customs Brokers and Forwarders Association of America, Inc., National Fisheries Institute, Regional Airline Association, Society of American Florists, and the U.S. Chamber of Commerce, *Letter to The Honorable Daniel Inouye and The Honorable Ted Stevens,* January 8, 2007, p. 1.
[34] Ibid.
[35] Transportation Security Administration, *Fiscal Year 2011 Congressional Justification, Aviation Security.*
[36] Andy Pasztor, Keith Johnson, and Daniel Michaels, "Focus on Cargo Security Steps," *Wall Street Journal,* November 1, 2010.
[37] Derek Kravitz and Ashley Halsey III, "U.S. Tightening Air Cargo Security," *Washington Post,* November 9, 2010.
[38] "TSA Says It Will Adhere to Cargo Screening Deadlines." *World Trade,* 20(12), December 2007, p. 10.
[39] Ibid.
[40] Thomas Frank, "Bill Would Order All Air Cargo Screened," *USA Today,* January 8, 2007.
[41] Air Transport Association, ATA Issue Brief: Air Cargo Security—The Airlines' View, Washington, DC: Air Transport Association.
[42] CRS analysis of airline industry economic data presented in: Air Transport Association, *Smart Skies: A Blueprint for the Future, 2007 Economic Report,* Washington, DC: Air Transport Association.
[43] Transportation Security Administration, *CCSP Overview—9/11 Act Screening Requirement.*
[44] Transportation Security Administration, *Fiscal Year 2011 Congressional Justification, Aviation Security.*
[45] Transportation Security Administration, *TSA Announces Key Milestone in Cargo Screening on Passenger Aircraft (Press Release).* August 2, 2010, http://www.tsa.gov/press/releases/2010/0802.shtm.
[46] Thomas Frank, Alan Levin, and Kevin Johnson, "Bomb Plot Shows Gaps in Screening of Air Cargo," *USA Today,* November 1, 2010.

[47] Transportation Security Administration. *NON-Sensitive Security Information (SSI) Version of the TSA Air Cargo Screening Technology List (ACSTL)*. July 16, 2010.

[48] Transportation Security Administration, *Fiscal Year 2011 Congressional Justification, Aviation Security*.

[49] Transportation Security Administration, *Fiscal Year 2010 Congressional Justification, Aviation Security*.

[50] Andy Pasztor, Keith Johnson, and Daniel Michaels, "Focus on Cargo Security Steps," *Wall Street Journal*, November 1, 2010.

[51] Dan A. Strellis, Tsahi Gozani, and John Stevenson, "Air Cargo Inspection Using Pulsed Fast Neutron Analysis," *International Topical Meeting on Nuclear Research Applications and Utilization of Accelerators, 4-8 May 2009 Vienna Austria*. International Atomic Energy Agency: Vienna, Austria.

[52] Derek Kravitz and Ashley Halsey III, "U.S. Tightening Air Cargo Security," *Washington Post*, November 9, 2010.

[53] "Electronic cargo security seals" *Frontline Solutions*, 3(6), 42 (June 2002).

[54] U.S. Government Accountability Office. *Aviation Security: Federal Action Needed to Strengthen Domestic Air Cargo Security*, October 2005, GAO-06-76.

[55] Transportation Security Administration, *Certified Cargo Screening Program Participant Newsletter*, August 20, 2010.

[56] National Commission on Terrorist Attacks Upon the United States. *The 9/11 Commission Report*.

[57] Boeing Commercial Airplanes. *747-400 Airplane Characteristics for Airport Handling*. D6-58326-1, December 2002.

[58] Transportation Security Administration, *Air Cargo Transportation Sector Network Management*.

[59] Transportation Security Administration, *Air Cargo Security Programs*.

In: Air Cargo Security
Editor: Pierre Turrión

ISBN: 978-1-62100-054-9
© 2012 Nova Science Publishers, Inc.

Chapter 3

TSA HAS MADE PROGRESS BUT FACES CHALLENGES IN MEETING THE STATUTORY MANDATE FOR SCREENING AIR CARGO ON PASSENGER AIRCRAFT[*]

United States Government Accountability Office

WHY GAO DID THIS STUDY

Billions of pounds of cargo are transported on U.S. passenger flights annually. The Department of Homeland Security's (DHS) Transportation Security Administration (TSA) is the primary federal agency responsible for securing the air cargo system. The 9/11 Commission Act of 2007 mandated DHS to establish a system to screen 100 percent of cargo flown on passenger aircraft by August 2010. As requested, GAO reviewed TSA's progress in meeting the act's screening mandate, and any related challenges it faces for both domestic (cargo transported within and from the United States) and inbound cargo (cargo bound for the United States). GAO reviewed TSA's policies and procedures, interviewed TSA officials and air cargo industry stakeholders, and conducted site visits at five U.S. airports, selected based on size, among other factors.

---

[*] This is an edited, reformatted and augmented version of the United States Government Accountability Office publication GAO-10-446, dated June 2010.

WHAT GAO RECOMMENDS

GAO recommends that TSA establish milestones for a staffing study, verify the accuracy of all reported screening data, develop a contingency plan for screening domestic cargo, and develop plans for meeting the mandate as it applies to inbound cargo. TSA partially concurred with verifying screening data and did not concur with developing a contingency plan because it did not believe such actions were feasible. GAO believes these recommendations remain valid, as discussed in this report. TSA agreed with all other recommendations.

WHAT GAO FOUND

TSA has made progress in meeting the air cargo screening mandate as it applies to domestic cargo, but faces challenges in doing so that highlight the need for a contingency plan. TSA has, for example, increased required domestic cargo screening levels from 50 percent in February 2009 to 75 percent in May 2010, increased the amount of cargo subject to screening by eliminating many domestic screening exemptions, created a voluntary program to allow screening to take place at various points in the air cargo supply chain, conducted outreach to familiarize industry stakeholders with screening requirements, and tested air cargo screening technologies. However, TSA faces several challenges in developing and implementing a system to screen 100 percent of domestic air cargo, and it is questionable, based on reported screening rates, whether 100 percent of such cargo will be screened by August 2010 without impeding the flow of commerce. For example, shipper participation in the voluntary screening program has been lower than targeted by TSA. In addition, TSA has not completed a staffing study to determine the number of inspectors needed to oversee the screening program. Because it is unclear how many industry stakeholders will join the program, TSA could benefit from establishing milestones to complete a staffing study to help ensure that it has the resources it needs under different scenarios. Moreover, TSA faces technology challenges that could affect its ability to meet the screening mandate. Among these, there is no technology approved by TSA to screen large pallets or containers of cargo, which suggests the need for alternative approaches to screening such cargo. TSA also does not verify the self-reported data submitted by screening participants. Several of these challenges suggest the need for a contingency plan, in case the agency's current initiatives are not successful in meeting the mandate without impeding the flow of commerce. However, TSA has not developed such a plan. Addressing these issues could better position TSA to meet the mandate.

TSA has made some progress in meeting the screening mandate as it applies to inbound cargo by taking steps to increase the percentage of screened inbound cargo—including working to understand the screening standards of other nations and coordinating with them to mutually strengthen their respective security efforts. Nevertheless, challenges remain and TSA does not expect to achieve 100 percent screening of inbound air cargo by the mandated August 2010 deadline. TSA officials estimate that air carriers are meeting the current mandated screening level of 50 percent of inbound cargo based on estimates rather than on actual data as required by law. Thus, TSA cannot verify if mandated screening levels are being met. In addition, the agency has not determined how it will eventually meet the screening mandate as it applies to inbound cargo; developing such a plan could better position TSA to assess its progress toward meeting the mandate.

ABBREVIATIONS

ATS	Automated Targeting System
CBP	U.S. Customs and Border Protection
CCSF	certified cargo screening facility
CCSP	Certified Cargo Screening Program
DHS	Department of Homeland Security
EC	European Commission
EDS	explosives detection system
EMD	electronic metal detection
ETD	explosives trace detection
IATA	International Air Transport Association
ICAO	International Civil Aviation Organization
IFR	interim final rule
S&T Directorate	Directorate for Science and Technology
TSA	Transportation Security Administration
TSI	transportation security inspector
ULD	unit load device

June 28, 2010
The Honorable Bennie G. Thompson
Chairman
Committee on Homeland Security
House of Representatives

The Honorable John D. Rockefeller, IV
Chairman
Committee on Commerce, Science, and Transportation
United States Senate

The Honorable Edward J. Markey
House of Representatives

In 2008, about 7.3 billion pounds of cargo was transported on U.S. passenger flights—approximately 58 percent of which was transported domestically (domestic cargo) and 42 percent of which was transported on flights arriving in the United States from a foreign location (inbound cargo).[1] The 2009 Christmas Day plot to detonate an explosive device during an international flight bound for Detroit demonstrates that terrorists continue to view passenger aircraft as attractive targets. According to the Transportation Security Administration (TSA), the security threat posed by terrorists introducing explosive devices in air cargo shipments is significant, and the risk and likelihood of such an attack directed at passenger aircraft is high.[2] Created by the November 2001 Aviation and Transportation Security Act, TSA is responsible for the screening of all passengers and property, including cargo, U.S. mail, and carry-on and checked baggage, transported on passenger aircraft.[3] In addition to TSA, U.S. Customs and Border Protection (CBP) plays a role in securing inbound cargo by selectively screening cargo upon its arrival in the United States.[4]

To help enhance the security of air cargo, the Implementing Recommendations of the 9/11 Commission Act of 2007 (9/11 Commission Act) mandated the Department of Homeland Security (DHS) to establish a system to physically screen 50 percent of cargo on passenger aircraft—including the domestic and inbound flights of foreign and U.S. passenger operations—by February 2009, and 100 percent of such cargo by August 2010.[5] The 9/11 Commission Act defines screening for purposes of the air cargo screening mandate as a physical examination or nonintrusive methods of assessing whether cargo poses a threat to transportation security.[6] The act also requires that such a system provide a level of security commensurate with the level of security for the screening of checked baggage. According to TSA, the mission of its air cargo security program is to secure the air cargo transportation system while not unduly impeding the flow of commerce. Although the mandate is applicable to both domestic and inbound cargo, TSA stated that it must address the mandate for domestic and inbound cargo through separate systems because of differences in its authority to regulate domestic and international air cargo industry stakeholders. This report will therefore address efforts to meet the screening mandate as it applies to domestic and inbound cargo separately.

You asked us to review TSA's progress in meeting the air cargo screening mandate. In response to this request, this report addresses the following questions:

1) What progress has TSA made in meeting the 9/11 Commission Act screening mandate as it applies to domestic air cargo, and what related challenges, if any, does TSA face?
2) What progress has TSA made in meeting the 9/11 Commission Act screening mandate as it applies to inbound air cargo, and what related challenges, if any, does TSA face?

To assess TSA's progress and challenges in implementing a system to meet the 9/11 Commission Act screening mandate as it applies to domestic cargo, we reviewed TSA's air cargo security policies and procedures, screening program documents, technology assessment procedures, TSA's Regulatory Activities Plan, the September 2009 air cargo interim final rule, and various DHS and industry stakeholder reports and testimony related to air cargo security, such as DHS Inspector General and industry reports.[7] In addition, we conducted site visits to four category X U.S. commercial airports and one category I U.S. commercial airport that process domestic and inbound air cargo.[8] We selected these airports based on the following criteria: airport size, passenger and air cargo volumes, location, and participation in TSA's screening program. At these airports, we observed screening operations and technologies and interviewed local TSA officials, airport management officials, and representatives from 7 air carriers, 24 freight forwarders, 3 shippers, and 2 handling agents to obtain their views on TSA's system to implement the screening mandate.[9] We selected these air carriers, freight forwarders, shippers, and handling agents based on input from TSA and from industry stakeholders. We also interviewed TSA air cargo program officials,

officials from DHS's Directorate for Science and Technology (S&T Directorate), TSA Office of Inspections officials, DHS Office of Inspector General officials, Department of Commerce officials, three air cargo industry consultants and experts, and representatives from six air cargo industry associations that represent a variety of air cargo industry stakeholders.[10] We selected these industry associations because they represent a large portion of the air cargo industry. We selected the industry consultants and experts based on their experience in the field of aviation security, and their recognition in the aviation security community. Our site visits and interviews with industry stakeholders were based on a nonprobability sample and are not generalizable to the entire air cargo industry. However, this sample allowed us to observe cargo screening operations and programs in various parts of the country with differing air cargo volumes and commodities, and thus provided important perspectives on TSA's air cargo screening program. We also analyzed TSA data on cargo screening levels and compliance violations from February 2009 through December 2009, and TSA data on compliance inspections from February 2009 through February 2010. We selected these date ranges because the air cargo screening requirement started in February 2009 and, at the time of our request, TSA data for cargo screening levels, compliance violations, and compliance inspections were only available through December 2009, December 2009, and February 2010, respectively. To assess the reliability of the data, we discussed quality control procedures with agency officials; reviewed TSA's data collection, entry, and analysis processes; and observed data entry and processing activities for screening data. We found the data to be sufficiently reliable to provide a general indication of cargo screening and compliance levels. We assessed TSA's efforts against criteria for successful project planning and standard practices for program management to determine if TSA's efforts evaluate staffing implications and include time frames and milestones.[11] In addition, we assessed TSA efforts against qualification testing procedures and time frames established by TSA to determine its progress in completing qualification testing of air cargo screening technologies. We also assessed TSA's screening verification procedures against the Office of Management and Budget's guidelines for ensuring information quality to determine if TSA reviews and substantiates the integrity of information before it is disseminated.[12] In addition, we assessed TSA's efforts against the agency's policies and procedures and criteria for successful project planning to determine if the agency's plan considers all phases of the project and includes schedules and deadlines.[13] Finally, we assessed TSA's plan for meeting the screening mandate as it applies to domestic cargo against criteria for comprehensive planning to determine whether it included contingency planning.[14]

To assess TSA's progress and challenges in implementing a system to meet the 9/11 Commission Act screening mandate as it applies to inbound air cargo, we reviewed TSA's air cargo policies and procedures and various DHS and industry stakeholder reports and testimony related to inbound air cargo security. We also interviewed local TSA officials, airport management officials, and representatives from seven air carriers at the five airports we visited to obtain their views on inbound cargo screening issues. In addition, we interviewed TSA air cargo program officials, including TSA international cargo inspectors, and representatives from six air cargo industry associations, and discussed TSA's plans with CBP officials.[15] We assessed TSA's plans for inbound cargo screening verification against standard practices for program management.[16] We also assessed TSA's plan for inbound cargo screening against criteria for successful project planning to determine if the agency's plan considers all phases of the project and includes schedules and deadlines.[17]

We conducted this performance audit from September 2008 through June 2010 in accordance with generally accepted government auditing standards. Those standards require that we plan and perform the audit to obtain sufficient, appropriate evidence to provide a reasonable basis for our findings and conclusions based on our audit objectives. We believe that the evidence obtained provides a reasonable basis for our findings and conclusions based on our audit objectives.

BACKGROUND

Approximately 16 percent of air cargo transported to, from, or within the United States is shipped on passenger aircraft, while the remainder is transported on all-cargo aircraft.[18] Overall, approximately 20 million pounds of cargo is transported on domestic and inbound passenger aircraft daily.[19] This cargo ranges in size from 1 pound to several tons and in type from perishable commodities to machinery. Air cargo can include such varied items as electronic equipment, automobile parts, clothing, medical supplies, fresh produce, and human remains. As seen in figure 1, cargo can be shipped in various forms, including unit load devices (ULD) that allow many packages to be consolidated into one large container or pallet that can be loaded onto an aircraft, wooden skids or crates, and individually wrapped/boxed pieces, known as loose or break bulk cargo.

Participants in the air cargo shipping process include shippers, such as individuals and manufacturers of various product types; freight forwarders, such as a company that accepts packages and ships them on behalf of individuals or manufacturers; air cargo handling agents, who process and load cargo onto aircraft on behalf of air carriers; and air carriers that load and transport cargo. A shipper may take or send its packages to a freight forwarder that in turn consolidates cargo from many shippers onto a master air waybill—a manifest of the consolidated shipment—and delivers the shipment to air carriers for transport. A shipper may also send freight by directly packaging and delivering it to an air carrier's ticket counter or sorting center, where the air carrier or a cargo handling agent will sort and load cargo onto the aircraft.

Source: GAO.

Figure 1. Various Types of Air Cargo.

TSA's responsibilities for securing air cargo include establishing security requirements governing domestic and foreign passenger air carriers that transport cargo, and domestic freight forwarders. TSA is also responsible for overseeing the implementation of air cargo security requirements by air carriers and freight forwarders through compliance inspections by transportation security inspectors (TSI)—staff within TSA responsible for aviation or cargo security inspections—and, in coordination with DHS's S&T Directorate, for guiding research and development of air cargo security technologies. Of the over $5.2 billion provided to TSA for aviation security in fiscal year 2010, approximately $123 million is for air cargo security as called for in the Conference Report for the DHS Appropriations Act, 2010. Of this amount, TSA was directed to use $15 million to test, evaluate, and deploy screening technologies; to expand canine teams operated by TSA by transferring 35 teams from those operated by local law enforcement; to deploy technologies to screen skids and pallets; and to increase the number of TSIs who oversee participants in the newly developed Certified Cargo Screening Program (CCSP)—a voluntary cargo screening program for freight forwarders, shippers, and other air cargo industry participants.[20] For fiscal year 2011, TSA has requested approximately $118 million for its air cargo security efforts.

U.S. and foreign air carriers, freight forwarders, and certified cargo screening facilities (CCSF)—industry stakeholders that have joined the CCSP—are responsible for implementing TSA security requirements, including maintaining a TSA-approved security program that describes the security policies, procedures, and systems the air carriers, freight forwarders, and CCSFs must implement to ensure compliance. These requirements include measures related to the acceptance, handling, and screening of cargo; training of employees in security and cargo screening procedures; testing for employee proficiency in cargo screening; and access to cargo areas and aircraft. Air carriers, freight forwarders, and CCSFs must also abide by security requirements imposed by TSA through security directives and amendments to security programs.

In addition to TSA, CBP and foreign governments play a role in securing inbound cargo. Unlike TSA, which requires screening prior to departure, CBP determines the admissibility of cargo into the United States and is authorized to inspect inbound air cargo for terrorists or weapons of mass destruction upon its arrival in the United States.[21] Foreign governments may also impose their own security requirements on cargo departing from their airports.

The 9/11 Commission Act specifies that air cargo screening methods include X-ray systems, explosives detection systems (EDS), explosives trace detection (ETD), explosives detection canine teams certified by TSA, physical search together with manifest verification, and any additional methods approved by the TSA Administrator.[22] However, solely performing a review of information about the contents of cargo or verifying the identity of the cargo's shipper does not constitute screening for purposes of satisfying the mandate. Figure 2 shows some approve d screening methods.

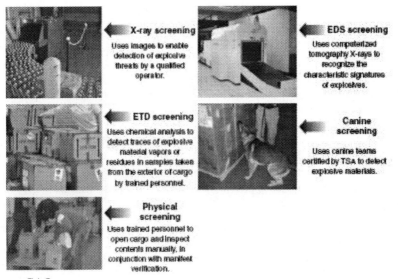

Source: GAO.

Figure 2. Approved Air Cargo Screening Methods.

TSA HAS MADE PROGRESS TOWARD SCREENING 100 PERCENT OF DOMESTIC CARGO TRANSPORTED ON PASSENGER AIRCRAFT, BUT REMAINING CHALLENGES HIGHLIGHT THE NEED FOR A CONTINGENCY PLAN

TSA has made progress in meeting the 9/11 Commission Act air cargo screening mandate as it applies to domestic cargo, and has taken several key steps in this effort, such as increasing the amount of domestic cargo subject to screening, creating a voluntary program—the CCSP—to allow screening to take place at various points along the air cargo supply chain, and taking steps to test air cargo screening technologies, among other actions. However, TSA faces several challenges in fully developing and implementing a system to screen 100 percent of domestic air cargo. For example, shipper participation in the CCSP has been lower than targeted by TSA. Furthermore, TSA lacks information to help ensure that it has the inspection resources it may need to provide effective oversight of CCSP entities. In addition, there is currently no technology approved or qualified by TSA to screen ULD pallets or containers, and TSA is working to complete qualification testing of several air cargo screening technologies to provide reasonable assurance of their effectiveness. Questions also exist about the reliability of the data used to calculate screening levels reported by TSA. Moreover, in-transit cargo—such as cargo that is transferred from an inbound to a domestic passenger flight—is not currently required to undergo physical screening. Finally, TSA has not developed a contingency plan to address CCSP participation and screening technology challenges, which could be implemented should TSA's current efforts not be sufficient to achieve the 100 percent screening mandate without impeding the flow of commerce.

Progress in Meeting the 100 Percent Screening Mandate as It Applies to Domestic Cargo

TSA has taken several steps to address the air cargo screening mandate.

TSA Increased the Amount of Domestic Cargo Subject to Screening

Effective October 1, 2008, several months prior to the first mandated deadline of 50 percent screening by February 2009, TSA established a requirement for 100 percent screening of nonexempt cargo transported on narrow-body passenger aircraft.[23] In 2008, narrow-body flights transported about 24 percent of all cargo on domestic passenger flights.[24] Effective February 1, 2009, pursuant to the 9/11 Commission Act, TSA also required air carriers to ensure the screening of 50 percent of all nonexempt air cargo transported on all passenger aircraft. Furthermore, effective May 1, 2010, air carriers were required to ensure that 75 percent of such cargo was screened. Although screening may be conducted by various entities, according to TSA regulations, each air carrier must ensure that the screening requirements are fulfilled. Furthermore, TSA eliminated or revised most of its screening exemptions for domestic cargo. For example, TSA eliminated the screening exemptions for palletized shrink-wrapped skids, effective February 2009, and for sealed pharmaceuticals and certain electronics, effective September 2009. As a result of the elimination of exemptions, most domestic cargo is now subject to TSA screening requirements. However, TSA is retaining several of the screening exemptions that apply to sensitive cargo.[25]

TSA Created a Voluntary Program to Facilitate Screening throughout the Air Cargo Supply Chain

Since TSA concluded that relying solely on air carriers to conduct screening would result in significant cargo backlogs and flight delays, TSA created the voluntary CCSP to allow screening to take place earlier in the shipping process, prior to delivering the cargo to the air carrier (see fig. 3). Under this decentralized approach, air carriers, freight forwarders, shippers, and other entities each play an important role in the screening of cargo. Under the CCSP, facilities at various points in the air cargo supply chain, such as shippers, manufacturers, warehousing entities, distributors, third-party logistics companies, and freight forwarders that are located in the United States, may voluntarily apply to TSA to become CCSFs. Once in the program, they are regulated by TSA. According to TSA officials, sharing screening responsibilities across the air cargo supply chain is expected to minimize the potential increases in cargo transit time, which could result if the majority of screening were conducted by air carriers at the airport. While the CCSP allows for a number of entities to conduct air cargo screening, according to TSA regulations, air carriers are responsible for ensuring that all domestic cargo transported on passenger aircraft is screened.[26] TSA officials stated that effective August 2010, unscreened domestic cargo would not be transported on passenger aircraft.

TSA initiated the CCSP at 18 U.S. airports that process high volumes of air cargo, and then expanded the program to all U.S. airports in early 2009.

CCSP participants were certified to begin screening cargo as of February 1, 2009. The shipper participants were regulated pursuant to an order, and the rules for freight forwarder participants were instituted through an amendment to their security programs.[27]

On September 16, 2009, TSA issued an interim final rule (IFR) that effective November 16, 2009, regulates the shippers, freight forwarders, and other entities participating in the CCSP.[28] According to the IFR, to become a CCSF, a facility's screening measures must be evaluated by TSA or a TSA-approved validation firm. Under its certification process, TSA requires each CCSF to demonstrate compliance with its security standards that include facility, personnel, procedural, perimeter, and information technology security.

Prior to certification, the CCSP applicant must submit for review and approval its training programs related to physical screening, facility access controls, and chain of custody, among other things. CCSF applicants must also implement TSA-approved security programs and appoint security coordinators before they can become certified. CCSFs must ensure that certain employees have undergone TSA-conducted security threat assessments; adhere to control measures for storing, handling, and screening cargo; screen cargo using TSA-approved methods; and implement chain of custody requirements.[29] Once certified, CCSFs must apply for recertification, including a new examination by TSA or a TSAapproved validator, every 36 months.

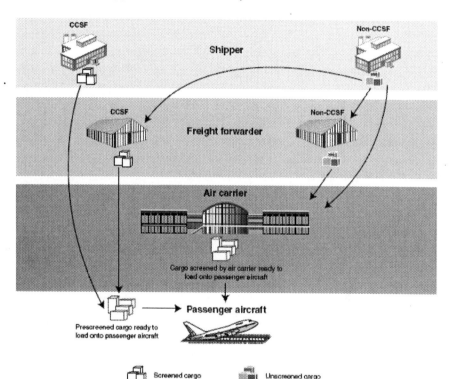

Sources: GAO (analysis), Art Explosion (clip art).
Note: After screening at a shipper CCSF, cargo may be transported to a freight forwarder for purposes other than screening, such as consolidation. However, this figure shows the locations of cargo screening and does not show cargo routes for purposes other than screening.

Figure 3. Flow of Cargo Screening at CCSFs and Air Carriers.

As part of the current program, and using TSA-approved screening methods, freight forwarder CCSFs must screen 50 percent of cargo being delivered to wide-body passenger aircraft and 100 percent of cargo being delivered to narrow-body passenger aircraft. According to TSA, although shipper CCSFs are not required to screen shipments to be delivered to a passenger aircraft, when they choose to conduct screening, such shipments must be screened at 100 percent.[30] In addition, each CCSF must deliver the screened cargo to air carriers while maintaining a secure chain of custody to prevent tampering with the cargo after it is screened. In fiscal year 2009, entities that were certified by TSA to participate in the CCSP were subject to annual inspections by TSIs and additional inspections at TSA's discretion. According to the 2010 TSI Regulatory Activities Plan, the agency plans to conduct at least two comprehensive inspections a year (i.e., a review of the implementation of all air cargo security requirements) for each CCSP participant. In addition, the agency plans to conduct more frequent inspections based on each entity's compliance history, among other factors.

TSA Is in the Process of Clarifying CCSF Screening and Training Requirements

During the course of our site visit conducted in July 2009, we identified two instances where CCSFs misinterpreted CCSP screening requirements. For example, a freight forwarder representative with whom we spoke stated that the freight forwarder's certified facilities have flexibility in the levels of cargo they have to screen, such as screening a percentage of cargo on some days while not screening any cargo on others. This interpretation is contrary to the view of senior TSA officials who are responsible for implementing the program, that freight forwarder CCSFs must screen a percentage of cargo on a daily basis, as required in their TSA-approved security programs. While the extent to which misinterpretation of the CCSP requirements occurs among program participants is unclear, the instances we identified indicated that freight forwarder CCSFs may not be applying TSA screening requirements consistently. When we brought this issue to the attention of a senior TSA official, he stated that the agency would benefit from strengthening and clarifying CCSP screening requirements. In March 2010, TSA officials reported that the agency has taken steps to clarify the requirements, though they did not specify what those steps were, and said the agency is planning to communicate these clarifications to relevant stakeholders.

During our site visits conducted in June and July 2009, we also observed two cases where training materials used by freight forwarder CCSFs to educate their employees on the use of technology to screen cargo may not have been consistent with TSA screening procedures. For example, one freight forwarder representative we interviewed during our site visit stated that his company compiled training materials on how to screen cargo with ETD technology from public information found on the Internet. However, TSA has no way of knowing whether the public information gathered from the Internet or from other sources used to develop training materials is reliable or consistent with TSA policies and procedures. After we brought this issue to the attention of TSA officials, TSA reported that the agency plans to clarify the CCSF training requirements regarding how to use technology to screen air cargo. Specifically, TSA plans to update these requirements in amendments to the freight forwarder CCSF policies and procedures. TSA officials also stated that the agency is considering providing CCSFs with a TSA-approved technology training package or a list of approved training vendors that CCSP participants can use to facilitate the training of their employees. The agency is in the early stages of this effort and has not yet developed time frames for when this effort will be completed.

TSA Is Conducting Outreach Efforts to Air Cargo Industry Stakeholders

Starting in September 2007, TSA began outreach to freight forwarders and subsequently expanded its outreach efforts to shippers and other entities to encourage participation in the CCSP. While industry participation in the CCSP is central to TSA's approach to spread screening responsibilities across the U.S. supply chain and, ultimately, meet the screening mandate, attracting shippers and freight forwarders to join the program is challenging because of the effect of the economic downturn on their resources and cargo volume, and the perception by some in the shipping and freight forwarder industry that screening costs and delays associated with air carriers conducting cargo screening will be minimal. TSA is focusing its outreach on particular industries, such as producers of perishable foods, pharmaceutical and chemical companies, and funeral homes, which may experience damage to their cargo if it is screened by a freight forwarder or an air carrier. TSA officials stated that they reach out to entities through a combination of conferences, outreach meetings, Internet presentations, and information posted in numerous trade association newsletters and on Web sites.

To enhance its outreach efforts, TSA established a team of 12 TSA field staff, or CCSP outreach coordinators, to familiarize industry with the air cargo screening mandate and the CCSP, as well as educate potential CCSP applicants on the program requirements.[31] In addition, outreach coordinators are responsible for certifying cargo screening facilities.[32] They visit the facilities of the CCSP applicants to assess their ability to meet program requirements and to address any deficiencies identified during the assessment. To complete the certification process, the outreach coordinator ensures that the facility has appropriate procedures and training in place to screen cargo. According to TSA officials, in February 2009, the agency also began using its air cargo TSIs in the field to conduct outreach. Officials from the one domestic passenger air carrier association and the one freight forwarder association with whom we spoke reported that TSA's staff has been responsive and helpful in answering questions about the program and providing information on CCSP requirements.[33]

TSA Is Taking Steps to Test Technologies for Screening Air Cargo

The 9/11 Commission Act specifies that the permitted methods of air cargo screening are X-ray systems, EDS, ETD, explosives detection canine teams, physical search together with manifest verification, and any additional methods approved by the TSA Administrator. However, TSA is responsible for determining which specific equipment models are authorized for use by industry stakeholders. We reported in March 2009 that TSA and DHS's S&T Directorate were pilot testing a number of technologies to screen air cargo.[34] For example, to test select screening technologies among CCSFs, TSA created the Air Cargo Screening Technology Pilot in January 2008, and selected some of the nation's largest freight forwarders to use these technologies and report on their experiences.[35] The screening that pilot participants perform counts toward meeting TSA screening requirements and in turn the air cargo screening mandate. In a separate effort, in July 2009, DHS's S&T Directorate completed the Air Cargo Explosives Detection Pilot Program that tested the performance of select baggage screening technologies for use in screening air cargo at three U.S. airports. TSA officials stated that the agency will be reviewing the pilot results and conducting additional testing on the technologies identified in the resulting S&T Directorate report.

Furthermore, TSA initiated a qualification process to test the technologies that it plans to allow air carriers and CCSP participants to use in meeting the August 2010 screening mandate against TSA technical requirements. In November 2008, in addition to the canine and physical search screening methods permitted by TSA to screen air cargo, as an interim measure, TSA issued to air carriers and CCSFs a list of X-ray, ETD, and EDS models that the agency approved for screening air cargo until August 3, 2010.[36] TSA approved these technologies based on its subject matter expertise and the testing and performance of these technologies in the checkpoint and checked baggage environments. In March 2009, TSA initiated a laboratory and field-based qualification testing process to ensure effectiveness of approved and other technologies in the air cargo environment and qualify them for use after August 3, 2010.[37] Once the initial stage of the qualification testing process is

Table 1. TSA and DHS Directorate for Science and Technology Programs to Test Technologies to Screen Air Cargo

Program	Description	Status
Air Cargo Screening Technology Pilot	Pilot participants—freight forwarder CCSFs and independent cargo screening facilities—operationally test ETD and X-ray technologies to determine their ability to screen high volumes of various cargo types and test chain of custody procedures. TSA provided the first round of participants with reimbursements up to $375,000 for purchasing technology, and the second with reimbursements up to $300,000.	As of December 31, 2009, 76 of 113 pilot participants were reporting screening data to TSA, such as cargo throughput, the number of equipment alarms triggered and resolved during screening, and chain of custody methods and their cost. TSA plans to complete the pilot in August 2010.
Air Cargo Explosives Detection Pilot	DHS tested the effectiveness, cost, and throughput of technologies and methods approved for screening checked baggage—EDS, ETD, standard X-ray machines, canine teams, and manual screening—in the air cargo environment.	In July 2009, DHS's S&T Directorate submitted the final report to Congress that identified some challenges related to applicability of technologies to the air cargo environment, such as the limited ability of ETD systems to detect threats in an air cargoenvironment, and recommended further technology testing.
Air Cargo Qualification Testing	TSA plans to test the capabilities of four technologies to identify a small amount of explosives in air cargo—X-ray, ETD, electronic metal detection (EMD), and EDS.[a] TSA determines the effectiveness of a particular technology through tests in laboratory and operational settings.	TSA reported that several X-ray technologieshave successfully passed initial qualification testing and announced which X-ray devices qualified in December 2009. In addition, TSA qualified EDS technologies based on past testing results, and will initiate qualification testing after August 2010. TSA planned to begin initial qualification testing for the ETD, EMD, and additional X-ray technologies in early 2010, and anticipates qualifying these technologies by summer of 2010.

Source: GAO analysis of information provided by TSA.
[a]EMD devices are capable of detecting metallic-based explosive components, such as wires, within a variety of perishable commodities at the cargo piece, parcel, and pallet levels.

accomplished, TSA's policy is to add successful candidates to a list of qualified products for industry stakeholders to utilize when purchasing technologies. For example, TSA added X-ray technologies to the list of qualified products in October 2009. TSA recommends that industry stakeholders purchase technologies from a list of qualified products because the technologies that do not pass the qualification testing process within 36 months of becoming approved are to be removed from a list of products authorized to screen air cargo. After issuing the list of qualified products, TSA plans to conduct additional stages of qualification testing and evaluation to determine the suitability of the screening equipment in an operational setting.

During the qualification testing process, TSA expects to utilize the results of the Air Cargo Screening Technology Pilot and conduct additional operational tests independent of the pilot. A description of several programs to test screening technologies for air cargo and their status is included in table 1.

TSA Expanded its Explosives Detection Canine Program

TSA has taken steps to expand the use of TSA-certified explosives detection canine teams. According to TSA, in fiscal year 2009, TSA canine teams screened over 145 million pounds of cargo, which represents a small portion of domestic air cargo.[38] As of February 2010, TSA had 113 dedicated air cargo screening canine teams—operating in 20 major airports—and is in the process of adding 7 additional canine teams.[39] TSA worked with air carriers to identify peak cargo delivery times, in order to schedule canine screening during times that would be most helpful to air carriers. TSA also deployed canine teams to assist the Pacific Northwest cherry industry during its peak harvest season from May through July 2009, to help air carriers and CCSFs handling this perishable commodity to meet the 50 percent screening requirement without disrupting the flow of commerce.

TSA Established a System to Verify that Screening is Being Conducted at the Mandated Levels

The agency established a system to collect and analyze data from screening entities to verify that requisite levels for domestic cargo are being met. Effective February 2009, TSA adjusted air carrier reporting requirements and added CCSF reporting requirements to include monthly screening reports on the number and weight of shipments screened. Based on reporting guidance issued by the agency, air carriers and CCSFs provided to TSA the first set of screening data in mid-March 2009, to be used as the basis for TSA's quarterly reports to Congress.[40] Under TSA's current process, screening data are manually reviewed and analyzed to determine if the screening is conducted at the mandated levels. According to TSA officials, the agency plans to transition from a manual process to automated data collection, review, and analysis by mid-2010. Based on these preliminary data, TSA has determined that over 50 percent of air cargo (by weight and number of shipments) transported on domestic passenger aircraft has been screened since the 50 percent requirement went into effect. For fiscal year 2009, TSA submitted its 2nd Quarter report, due in May 2009, on October 2, 2009, verifying these screening levels.[41] The 3rd Quarter report, due in August 2009, was submitted on January 7, 2010. The 4th Quarter report, due in November 2009, is undergoing Office of Management and Budget review.

TSA is developing a covert testing program to identify security vulnerabilities in the air cargo environment. TSA conducts undercover, or covert, tests that are designed to approximate techniques that terrorists may use in order to identify vulnerabilities in the people, processes, and technologies that make up the aviation security system. TSA officials reported that the agency plans to carry out a covert testing program for the air cargo environment in two phases and will conduct tests at shipper, freight forwarder, and air carrier facilities.[42] Both phases are scheduled to begin in 2010. TSA is in the early stages of developing the testing protocols and thus has not yet established a timetable for their completion. According to TSA officials, the agency plans to use the results of these tests to identify and remedy vulnerabilities in the air cargo system.

In addition, TSA operates a risk-based Air Cargo Vulnerability Assessment program to identify weaknesses and potential vulnerabilities in the domestic air cargo supply chain. As of March 2010, TSA has conducted assessments at 33 U.S. airports and completed assessments at all domestic category X airports in December 2009. After completing these assessments, TSA stated that it will utilize the results to refine policy for air cargo security.

Challenges in Meeting the Screening Mandate as It Applies to Domestic Air Cargo

TSA faces industry participation, oversight, technology, and other challenges, and could benefit from a contingency plan to identify alternatives for meeting the air cargo screening mandate

Lower-than-Targeted Levels of Shipper Participation in the CCSP Could Affect TSA Progress in Meeting the Screening Mandate

Although TSA is relying on the voluntary participation of industry stakeholders to meet the screening mandate, some stakeholders have not participated in the program at targeted levels. As shown in figure 4, TSA officials have estimated that an ideal mix of screening to achieve the 100 percent mandate as it applies to domestic cargo without impeding the flow of commerce would be about one-third of cargo weight screened by air carriers, one-third by freight forwarders, and one-third by shippers and independent CCSFs.[43] The air carrier portion includes a small amount of screening by TSA canine teams and by TSIs at the smaller category II through IV airports. TSA officials emphasized that this estimated ideal mix is not precise but is intended to illustrate that balanced industry participation is needed to achieve the goals of the program.

However, as of March 2010, the percentage of cargo reported as screened by shipper and independent CCSFs remained at 2 percent—far lower than the 33 percent TSA cites as the portion these entities should ideally screen. To achieve TSA's ideal mix of screening by August 2010, shipper and independent CCSF screening efforts would need to increase by over sixteenfold. Moreover, as shown in figure 4, the total percentage of reported screened cargo rose on average by less than a percentage point per month (from 59 to 68 percent) from February 2009 through March 2010.[44] At these rates, it is questionable whether TSA's screening system will achieve 100 percent screening of domestic cargo by August 2010 without impeding the flow of commerce. Effective May 1, 2010, TSA requires that 75 percent of air cargo transported on passenger aircraft be screened. However, even if this requirement is met, an additional 25 percent of domestic passenger air cargo would still need to be screened in the 3 months prior to the August 2010 deadline, including some of the most challenging types of cargo to screen, such as ULD pallets and containers.

In March 2010, TSA officials stated that they surveyed current CCSFs and CCSP applicants to estimate these air cargo industry stakeholders' capacity for screening domestic cargo—this could help predict the industry's success in meeting the 100 percent screening deadline.[45] According to TSA officials, the survey indicated that current and prospective CCSFs have the potential capacity needed to screen cargo so that short-term delays at only the nation's 18 major airports will result when the 100 percent deadline goes into effect.

However, TSA did not have supporting documentation of the survey's methodology or results. Thus, we were unable to independently verify TSA's assertions or the rigor of TSA's methodology and analysis. For example, it is unclear whether TSA's survey and estimation took into account cargo that is inherently difficult to screen, such as ULD pallets or containers, or whether it focused primarily on loose cargo that is being screened with relative ease. It is also important to note that having the potential capacity to screen air cargo does not ensure that this capacity will be fully utilized to meet the air cargo screening mandate.

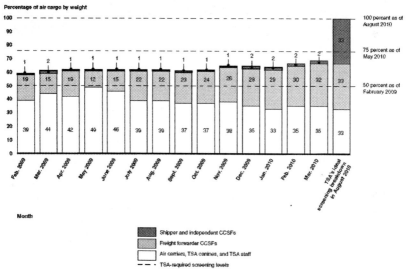

Source: GAO analysis of TSA screening data and information.

Notes: TSA was not able to provide us with screening data more recent than March 2010. We found these industry-reported data to be sufficiently reliable to provide a general indication of cargo screening levels. The reported and ideal screening breakdown percentages have been rounded to the nearest percentage point. The ideal screening breakdown percentages actually sum to 100 percent. The reported screening percentages for December 2009 actually sum to 64 percent, for February 2010 actually sum to 66 percent, and for March 2010 actually sum to 68 percent.

Figure 4. TSA's Reported and Ideal Screening Percentage Breakdowns for Domestic Air Cargo Transported on Passenger Aircraft from February 2009 through March 2010.

In addition, TSA officials stated that they did not develop milestones to monitor CCSP progress because air cargo screening by industry stakeholders is driven by market forces that are beyond the control of the government and are impossible to forecast. Further, according to TSA officials, if the CCSP participants cannot contribute the amount of screening needed to achieve 100 percent screening by the August 2010 deadline, the air carriers will be responsible for screening any remaining unscreened cargo at the airport or ensuring that it does not fly on a passenger aircraft. However, according to officials from the two major air carrier industry associations and the one freight forwarder association with whom we spoke, if the volume of cargo is too great for air carriers to handle, it could significantly disrupt the air cargo industry because of delays from cargo screening at the airport and the shift of unscreened cargo to alternate modes of transportation, such as all-cargo aircraft or trucks. Officials from one major air carrier industry association further noted that this would particularly be a problem if the volume of large cargo configurations—such as ULD pallets or containers—that air carriers have to disassemble and screen is too great for air carriers to handle. As discussed earlier, according to TSA officials, these disruptions will be short term and limited to 18 major airports. However, these 18 airports process 65 percent of domestic cargo transported on passenger aircraft, which suggests that disruptions may be substantial. TSA's rationale for creating the CCSP, and spreading screening responsibilities throughout the supply chain, is to mitigate the risks of these sorts of disruptions. However, these CCSP participation challenges demonstrate that TSA could benefit from developing a contingency plan, as we will discuss later, should it become clear that participation rates are not sufficient to achieve the screening mandate without impeding the flow of commerce.

Regulatory and Economic Factors May Affect Industry Participation in the CCSP

According to TSA officials, some shippers have expressed interest in the CCSP, particularly those in certain industries, such as the pharmaceutical industry, whose cargo would be compromised if opened and screened by others. However, TSA and industry officials reported that several factors, such as lack of economic and regulatory incenti5ves, are contributing to low shipper participation levels. For example, TSA and the freight forwarder industry association official with whom we spoke reported that flexibility in applying current TSA screening requirements—such as the ability to screen only easier-to-screen cargo and leave more challenging cargo unscreened—and low cargo volumes have minimized screening-related cargo delays and cargo screening costs. For example, until the 100 percent screening mandate goes into effect in August 2010, air carriers may be able to meet TSA screening requirements by screening mostly loose or break-bulk cargo and not the more challenging and time-consuming cargo, such as ULD pallets and containers or large wooden crates.

Officials from the domestic passenger air carrier association and freight forwarder industry association with whom we spoke reported that because of the difficult economic environment and flexibility stakeholders have in choosing what cargo to screen, most air carriers are not currently charging freight forwarders or shippers for cargo screening in order to attract and retain customers. As a result, TSA and the domestic passenger air carrier and freight forwarder industry association officials we interviewed stated that many shippers and freight forwarders are not incurring significant screening costs from air carriers, which decreases the financial pressure on the entities to join the CCSP and invest resources into screening cargo, factors that are making TSA's outreach efforts more challenging.

Moreover, the freight forwarder industry association official with whom we spoke stated that some industry participants may not be able to join the program because of potential program costs. TSA has estimated in the IFR that the total cost for industry participation in the CCSP will be about $2.2 billion over a 10-year period, though the agency has not provided per capita cost estimates for industry. The freight forwarder industry association official with whom we spoke reported that business models of large freight forwarders require them to purchase time-saving screening equipment so that screeners can avoid physically opening and examining each piece of cargo.[46] However, TSA and this industry official agreed that the majority of small freight forwarders—which handle 20 percent of the cargo but make up 80 percent of the total number of freight forwarding companies—would likely find the costs of joining the CCSP, including acquiring expensive technology, hiring additional personnel, conducting additional training, and making facility improvements, prohibitive. Moreover, shippers that distribute products from other companies in addition to or instead of their own manufactured goods might also find it cost prohibitive to join the CCSP if they were required to purchase screening equipment. However, TSA officials stated that most shippers can incorporate physical searches into their packing and shipping processes to satisfy TSA screening requirements, thereby avoiding such capital expenses.

TSA established the Air Cargo Screening Technology Pilot program to make some financial reimbursement available to large freight forwarders and independent CCSFs for the technology they have purchased. TSA reported that it targeted high-volume facilities (i.e., facilities processing at least 200 ULDs or their equivalent weight of approximately 500,000 pounds annually, shipments annually that contain cargo consolidated from multiple shippers) for the pilot in order to have the greatest effect in helping industry achieve the new screening requirements. As of February 2010, 113 CCSFs have joined the pilot. However, the majority of CCSFs do not ship large enough volumes of consolidated cargo to qualify for the pilot, and thus cannot receive funding for technology or other related costs. The freight forwarder industry association official with whom we spoke expressed concerns regarding the cost of purchasing and maintaining screening equipment. In response to concerns of medium and small freight forwarders that they might not be able to join the program because of potential costs, TSA officials stated that the agency is allowing independent CCSFs to join the CCSP and screen cargo on behalf of freight forwarders and shippers. In this scenario, small freight forwarders or shippers would not need to join the CCSP or purchase technology to avoid screening at the airport, but could send their cargo for a fee to an independent CCSF for screening. However, TSA and the freight forwarder industry association official with whom we spoke stated that the independent CCSFs are having difficulties attracting clientele in the current depressed economic environment. According to these officials, shippers and other supply chain participants might use independent CCSFs to screen their cargo once the 100 percent screening requirement goes into effect, if cargo volumes increase before that time or if cargo experiences screening delays. Many of the challenges in attracting industry participation in the CCSP are outside of TSA's control, and agency officials stated that they are working to raise industry awareness of the benefits of joining the program through TSA's ongoing outreach efforts.

Determining the Level of Inspection Resources Needed to Effectively Oversee CCSP Entities Could Help TSA Efforts to Ensure the Program's Success

While TSA has amended its Regulatory Activities Plan to include inspections of CCSP participants, the agency has not completed its staffing study to assess its staffing needs and determine how many inspectors will be necessary to provide oversight of the additional program participants when the 100 percent screening mandate goes into effect.[47] TSA's compliance inspections range from reviews of the implementation of all air cargo security requirements (i.e., comprehensive) to a more frequent review of at least one security requirement (i.e., supplemental). TSA recognized that the creation of the CCSP added additional regulated entities to TSI oversight responsibilities, and incorporated additional inspection requirements into the TSI Regulatory Activities Plan. Beginning under the plan for fiscal year 2009, TSIs are to perform compliance inspections of new regulated entities, such as shippers and manufacturers, that voluntarily become CCSFs, as well as new inspections of freight forwarder CCSFs that are in addition to inspections related to their freight forwarder responsibilities. In addition to their pre-CCSP inspection responsibilities, under the plan for fiscal year 2010, TSIs are to conduct at least two comprehensive inspections a year for each CCSF to verify compliance with the program requirements.[48]

As of March 2010, TSA had 1,258 TSIs, of which 533 were dedicated cargo TSIs or cargo TSI canine handlers. The agency was authorized 50 new cargo TSI positions in fiscal year 2010 to provide additional oversight of CCSP operations. TSA officials reported that they have developed an interim program-level methodology to allocate these TSIs to airports based on CCSP participation and cargo volume, among other factors, and that they believe they have a sufficient number of inspectors to ensure compliance with the CCSP. However, the agency staffing study, which would determine the resources necessary to provide CCSP oversight, is not yet complete. According to TSA, the agency's staffing study is continuing through fiscal year 2010 and is therefore not yet available to provide guidance in helping to plan for inspection resources needed to provide oversight.

Complicating TSA efforts to determine the level of inspection resources needed is the extent to which market forces will affect CCSP participation and therefore how many additional CCSFs will join the program and thus be subject to TSA's inspection requirements. As of March 1, 2010, 583 entities had joined the CCSP. Given this level of participation, TSA's TSI workforce must conduct at least 1,166 comprehensive inspections of CCSFs per year. According to our analysis of TSA data, in the next year, inspectors will need to at least double their comprehensive inspections of CCSFs to reach this target.[49] Moreover, according to our analysis of TSA data, approximately one-quarter to one-third of CCSFs have not received a comprehensive inspection.[50]

According to TSA officials, CCSFs that have never been inspected are deemed high risk and must be inspected by the following quarter. However, since TSA officials anticipate that CCSP participation will continue to grow, and that there could be a groundswell in CCSP participants as the 100 percent screening deadline approaches, TSIs may be challenged in dealing with the increased inspection workload once the screening mandate goes into effect in August 2010. For example, the IFR stated that about 5,600 entities are expected to join the CCSP. Based on these figures, TSA would be required to conduct 11,200 comprehensive inspections annually. TSA officials questioned the accuracy of this estimate, and stated that for workforce planning purposes, a more realistic near-term estimate for the number of CCSFs TSA is expected to oversee is the number of current CCSFs and CCSP applicants. However, TSA did not provide us this total figure. Moreover, as discussed earlier, TSA does not know how many CCSFs will join the program in the future, and does not plan to estimate the number of CCSP participants needed to meet the 100 percent screening mandate. Without this key information, it will be difficult for TSA to obtain a reasonable estimate of the number of inspectors that will be needed to oversee the CCSP participants— highlighting the need for a staffing study that considers various scenarios.

In addition, according to TSA data, of the CCSF compliance inspections conducted from February 1, 2009, to December 29, 2009, some resulted in at least one violation of CCSF security requirements—and a percentage of these violations were screening related.[51] Having the resources needed to provide effective oversight will be critical to ensuring that CCSFs are comprehensively inspected soon after being certified, in order to identify violations and provide TSA with some assurance that CCSFs are conducting their new screening activities in accordance with TSA requirements.

As we reported in prior work, successful project planning should evaluate staffing implications.[52] Since fiscal year 2008, TSA officials have reported on a planned TSI staffing study, and air cargo program officials stated that this study would include an analysis of the resources necessary to provide CCSP oversight and would incorporate information on the number of CCSFs to be inspected in order to assess workforce needs. Officials stated in March 2010 that the study would continue through fiscal year 2010. However, the agency has not established an estimated completion date or interim milestones (i.e., dates and related tasks) for completion of the study, and officials did not provide an explanation for why this has not yet occurred. Standard practices for program management call for the establishment of time frames and milestones.[53] Creating time frames with milestones could help ensure completion of the staffing study, the results of which should better position

TSA to ensure that the inspectors it needs are in place in order to oversee effective CCSF implementation of TSA security requirements.

TSA and Industry Stakeholders Face Challenges in Screening Certain Types of Cargo, and TSA Is Working to Test the Effectiveness of Screening Technologies

TSA faces challenges related to screening certain types of cargo, qualification testing of technology, and securing the chain of custody.

Screening Cargo in ULD Pallets and Containers

There is currently no technology approved or qualified by TSA to screen cargo once it is loaded onto a ULD pallet or container—both of which are common means of transporting air cargo on wide-body passenger aircraft. Cargo transported on wide-body passenger aircraft makes up 76 percent of domestic air cargo shipments transported on passenger aircraft.[54] Prior to May 1, 2010, canine screening was the only screening method, other than physical search, approved by TSA to screen such cargo. Canine teams were deployed to 20 airports to assist air carriers with such screening. In addition, the 2009 S&T Directorate technology pilot study reported canine teams to be an effective method of screening ULD pallets and containers, but it identified an urgent need to find other effective methods for screening such cargo because of the shortage of available canine teams. TSA officials, however, still have some concerns about the effectiveness of the canine teams, and effective May 1, 2010, the agency no longer allows canine teams to be used for primary screening of ULD pallets and containers. Instead, TSA allows canines to conduct primary screening of only loose cargo and 48-by-48-inch cargo skids. Canine teams still may be used for secondary screening of ULD pallets and containers; however, secondary screening does not count toward meeting the air cargo screening mandate.

TSA officials reported that they have conducted preliminary assessments of technologies that are capable of screening ULD pallets and containers but that commercially available technologies do not exist that effectively detect explosives in the amounts described in TSA standards. TSA officials stated that TSA continues to work with technology vendors on developing technologies that will be able to effectively screen ULD pallets and containers. In the interim, TSA officials indicated that the agency is encouraging industry stakeholders through the CCSP to screen such cargo earlier in the supply chain, before cargo is consolidated. However, according to representatives of the two major air carrier industry associations and the one freight forwarder association with whom we spoke, technology available to screen consolidated or palletized cargo, including cargo in a ULD, is critical in meeting the 100 percent screening mandate given that such cargo represents a primary means for transporting cargo transported on passenger aircraft. Moreover, while industry participation in the CCSP may help ensure that screening takes place earlier in the supply chain, which will help alleviate the challenges posed by ULD pallets and containers, to date, far fewer shippers have joined the CCSP than TSA anticipated, and these ULD pallets and containers currently make up about 76 percent of domestic air cargo transported on passenger aircraft, with no efficient method to screen them. These technology challenges suggest the need for TSA to consider alternative approaches to meet the screening mandate without unduly affecting the flow of commerce, as we will discuss later.

TSA Is Working to Qualify Some Air Cargo Screening Technologies

In addition, TSA is working to complete qualification testing of air cargo screening technologies; thus, until all stages of qualification testing are concluded, the agency may not have reasonable assurance that the technologies that air carriers and program participants are currently allowed to use to screen air cargo are effective. Qualification tests are designed to verify that a technology system meets the technical requirements specified by TSA. TSA qualified several X-ray technologies for purchase by industry stakeholders based on initial test results and qualified EDS technologies based on their past performance in other testing processes. TSA has not yet qualified ETD and other X-ray technologies that TSA allows program participants to use to screen air cargo. Once these technologies have been added to the list of qualified products, the agency is to conduct additional stages of qualification testing. TSA officials expressed confidence in the initial qualification test results because the commercial off-the-shelf technologies being used for cargo screening have a proven record in the passenger checkpoint and checked baggage environments. However, TSA acknowledged that if the results of additional stages of qualification testing do not meet its technical requirements, these technologies can be removed from the list of qualified products.

Furthermore, because of the mandated deadlines, TSA is conducting qualification testing to determine which screening technologies are effective at the same time that air carriers are using these technologies to meet the mandated requirement to screen air cargo transported on passenger aircraft. For example, according to TSA, ETD technology will undergo the initial phase of qualification testing in the air cargo environment in 2010, although many air carriers and CCSFs are currently using it to screen air cargo. Moreover, technology reports and TSA officials disagree as to the effectiveness of ETD technology. For example, a pilot program completed by DHS's S&T Directorate in July 2009 found that the ability of ETD technology to detect explosive threats in cargo by sampling the external surfaces of cargo shipments for explosive residue— the standard ETD protocol required by TSA—is poor. According to TSA officials, external sampling of cargo shipments is a method of screening preferred by freight forwarders and air carriers in order to avoid opening all cargo pieces, which can result in possible damage to the contents and significantly greater screening time. The pilot program recommended further research to evaluate the applicability and efficacy of external sampling using ETD systems, as well as other screening systems, to detect threats, such as explosives, in air cargo. However, TSA officials disputed the findings of this S&T Directorate study. They also stated that other S&T Directorate reports support the acceptance of ETD technology; however, we were unable to review these reports since this information was provided late in our review.[55] The lack of consensus within DHS regarding the effectiveness of ETD technology in the air cargo environment suggests the need for additional study.

Although TSA officials stated that simultaneous testing and use of technology by the industry is not ideal, they noted that this was necessary to meet the screening deadlines mandated by the 9/11 Commission Act. While we recognize that certain circumstances, such as mandated deadlines, require expedited deployment of technologies, our prior work has shown that programs with immature technologies have experienced significant cost and schedule growth.[56] For example, we reported in October 2009 that TSA deployed a passenger checkpoint technology—the explosives trace portal (ETP)—to airports without proving its performance in an operational environment, contrary to TSA's acquisition guidance, which recommends such testing.[57] The agency purchased hundreds of these machines but was forced to halt their deployment because of performance, maintenance, and installation issues. All but 9 ETPs have been withdrawn from airports and 18 remain in inventory. TSA determined that the remainder of the ETPs was excess capacity.

Since TSA plans to issue a list of qualified technologies before all stages of qualification testing are complete, the industry lacks assurance that the qualification status of technologies established by TSA for use after August 2010 will not change. Further testing could result in modifications to the list of qualified technologies authorized for use after August 3, 2010, and to the list of technologies approved by TSA for use through January 2012.

TSA has reserved the option of revising the status of any particular technology or system in the event that its performance in an operational environment indicates that it is losing effectiveness or suitability to an unacceptable degree as it ages or that constantly evolving threats require new detection capabilities. The domestic passenger air carrier and freight forwarder industry association officials with whom we spoke expressed concerns about purchasing technology from the lists of approved and qualified technologies that are subject to change. TSA officials stated that the agency is accelerating its testing timeline and the release of the qualification testing results for these technologies to meet the screening deadlines mandated by Congress. For example, TSA originally planned to release the X-ray qualification results after completing all stages of qualification testing. Because of approaching deadlines, however, in December 2009 and based on initial test results, TSA announced the qualification of certain X-ray technologies. It is unclear, however, whether the challenges TSA faces in issuing a list of fully qualified screening technologies will allow the industry to make informed decisions about technology purchases to meet the screening requirements of the 9/11 Commission Act.

Securing the Chain of Custody in the Air Cargo Shipping Process

With regard to technology, another area of concern in the transportation of air cargo is the chain of custody between the various entities that handle and screen cargo before it is loaded onto an aircraft. TSA officials stated that the agency has taken steps to analyze the chain of custody under the CCSP, and has issued cargo procedures to all entities involved in the CCSP to ensure that the chain of custody of cargo is secure. We found that the procedures issued by TSA to the CCSFs include guidance on when and how to secure cargo with tamper-evident technology, but do not include standards for the types of technologies that should be used. TSA officials noted that they are in the process of compiling a list of existing tamper-evident technologies and their manufacturers. Once the list is complete, TSA plans to test and evaluate these technologies and issue recommendations to the industry. TSA has not yet set any time frames for issuing such recommendations because, according to TSA officials, they need to explore cost-effective technologies first.

Securing the chain of custody for cargo screened under the CCSP takes on additional significance in light of the DHS Inspector General's 2009 report findings that TSA could improve its efforts to secure air cargo during ground handling and transportation.[58] For example, the report determined that industry personnel were accessing, handling, or transporting cargo without the required background checks. In addition, the report stated that TSA's inspection process has not been effective in ensuring that requirements for securing air cargo during ground transportation are understood or followed. In response to the DHS Inspector General report, TSA concurred with the recommendation to improve the security threat assessment process and stated that the IFR requires recordkeeping for security threat assessments. TSA also concurred with the DHS Inspector General recommendation to revise the Regulatory Activities Plan to allow more time for inspectors to provide support and education to regulated entities to ensure that air cargo security requirements are understood and implemented. TSA reported that the fiscal year 2010 Regulatory Activities Plan addresses this concern.

TSA Is Working to Verify that Domestic Screening Is Being Conducted at the Requisite Levels, but Questions Exist about the Reliability of the Reported Data

While TSA reported to Congress that industry achieved the February 2009 50 percent screening deadline as it applies to domestic cargo, questions exist about the reliability of the screening data, which are self-reported by industry representatives. TSA has been collecting and analyzing data from screening entities, such as air carriers, freight forwarders, and shippers, since March 2009 to verify that domestic screening is being conducted at the requisite levels. As of March 2010 TSA reported that 68 percent of domestic cargo by weight had been screened. After receiving data from screening entities, TSA performs preliminary data quality checks, such as viewing the data to identify missing or duplicate values. However, TSA does not have a mechanism to verify the accuracy of the data reported by the industry.[59] TSA stated that as part of its compliance inspections for air carriers and CCSFs, TSIs check industry screening logs—which include information on how and by whom a specific shipment was screened—to verify that the required screening levels have been met. However, TSIs do not compare these screening logs to the reports that air carriers and CCSFs submit to TSA with their screening levels because according to senior TSA officials, such comparisons would be significantly burdensome to the industry. Specifically, senior TSA officials stated that the air carrier reports do not contain details on specific shipments, thus verification is not feasible. However, senior TSA officials agreed that it is important to verify the accuracy of the data reported by the industry through random checks or other practical means, and that greater coordination among TSA program and compliance officials is necessary to ensure that these checks are taking place. The Office of Management and Budget's guidelines for ensuring quality of information call for agencies to develop procedures for reviewing and substantiating the integrity of information before it is disseminated.[60] Given that TSA uses the data submitted by screening entities to verify its compliance with the mandate as it applies to domestic cargo and to report to Congress, ensuring the accuracy of the self-reported data is of particular significance. In order to do this, TSA could, for example, adopt a program similar to CBP's compliance measurement program, which is used to determine the extent to which importers are in compliance with laws and regulations. As part of this program, CBP conducts regular quality reviews to ensure accuracy in findings and management oversight to validate results. Verifying the accuracy of the self-reported screening data could better position TSA in providing reasonable assurance that screening is being conducted at reported levels.

TSA Requirements Do Not Ensure that In-Transit Cargo Transferred from an Inbound to a Domestic Flight Is Physically Screened

Cargo that has already been transported on one leg of a passenger flight—known as in-transit cargo—may be subsequently transferred to another passenger flight without undergoing screening. For example, cargo transported on an inbound flight, a significant percentage of which is exempt from screening, can be transferred to a domestic flight without physical screening.[61] According to TSA officials, though the agency does not have a precise figure, industry estimates suggest that about 30 percent of domestic cargo is transferred from an inbound flight. According to TSA officials, the agency had determined that additional screening of this cargo was not required, in part because an actual flight mimics a screening method that until recently was approved for use.[62]

A senior TSA official also stated that because in-transit cargo transferred from an inbound flight has flown under a TSA-approved passenger aircraft security program, it is in compliance with TSA screening requirements. However, a significant amount of inbound cargo is exempt from screening.[63] In contrast, TSA's policies and procedures require all cargo flown on domestic flights to be screened at 75 percent, effective May 1, 2010. As a result, despite being flown under a TSA-approved security program, in-transit cargo originating in foreign countries is not required to be screened at the same levels as cargo transported on domestic flights. Therefore, TSA lacks assurance that this cargo is being screened in accordance with 9/11 Commission Act required screening levels.

In response to our questions as part of this review, TSA officials stated that transporting in-transit cargo without screening could pose a vulnerability, but as of February 2010, the agency was not planning to require in-transit cargo transferred from an inbound flight to be physically screened because of the logistical difficulties associated with screening cargo that is transferred from one flight to another. However, these logistical difficulties could be minimized if more cargo were screened prior to departure from a foreign location. Thus, addressing the potential security vulnerability posed by in-transit cargo is directly linked to TSA's efforts to secure and screen inbound cargo, which is discussed later in this report. Although TSA officials stated that they plan to explore measures for screening in-transit cargo in the future, these officials did not provide documentation of these measures or information on milestones for their implementation. A successful project plan—such as a plan that would be used to establish such measures—should consider all phases of the project, and clearly state schedules and deadlines.[64] Developing a plan with milestones that addresses how in-transit cargo will be screene d in accordance with 9/11 Commission Act requirements could better position TSA to meet the mandate and reduce potential vulnerabilities associated with such cargo.

Contingency Planning Could Help TSA Identify Alternatives for Meeting the Air Cargo Screening Mandate

Although TSA faces industry participation and technology challenges that could impede the CCSP's success and the agency's efforts to meet the 100 percent screening mandate, the agency has not developed a contingency plan that considers alternatives to address these challenges. As discussed earlier, as of December 2009, the percentage of cargo screened by shipper and independent CCSFs remains far lower than the percentage TSA cites as the portion these entities should ideally screen. Without adequate CCSP participation, industry may not be able to screen enough cargo prior to its arrival at the airport to maintain the flow of commerce while meeting the mandate. Likewise, without technology solutions for screening cargo in a ULD pallet or container—which makes up about 76 percent of cargo transported on domestic passenger aircraft—industry may not have the capability to effectively screen 100 percent of air cargo without affecting the flow of commerce. TSA is continuing to work with vendors on developing technology to effectively screen ULD pallets and containers, and in the interim, is encouraging industry stakeholders as part of the CCSP to screen such cargo earlier in the supply chain, before it is loaded onto ULDs, but such actions will not ensure that such cargo is screened. We have previously reported that a comprehensive planning process, including contingency planning, is essential to help an agency meet current and future capacity challenges.[65] Alternatives could include, but are not limited to, mandating CCSP participation for certain members of the air cargo supply chain—instead of relying on their voluntary participation—and requiring the screening of some or all cargo before it is loaded onto ULD pallets and containers. Developing a contingency plan that addresses the participation and technology challenges that could impede the screening program's success, and identifies alternate or additional security measures to implement in case the program is unable to effectively facilitate the screening of sufficient amounts of cargo prior to reaching air carriers at the airport, could better position TSA to meet the requirements in the air cargo screening mandate.

    With regard to the consideration of alternatives to the CCSP, TSA reported that it considered requiring air carriers to bear the full burden of the screening mandate and also considered creating TSA-operated screening facilities at airports, but determined that both strategies would result in severe disruptions to commerce because of limited airport space for screening. Representatives of the two major air carrier associations with whom we spoke stated that additional TSA screening by canine teams would be helpful, and industry stakeholders have also identified the option of using private companies to provide canine screening in order to expand the number of canines available for screening. According to TSA, the agency is considering whether to pursue this option because of concerns regarding certification of canines that have not been trained by TSA and are not handled by TSA staff. In addition, TSA officials stated that the agency does not plan to provide canine teams as a long-term primary screening method once the CCSP grows and industry develops more capacity to screen cargo, as industry, not the federal government, is responsible for screening air cargo under TSA's regulations.

TSA officials also stated that alternative or additional screening measures will not be necessary because unscreened cargo will simply not be transported on passenger aircraft, that is, "will not fly." Although this approach would ensure that 100 percent of air cargo transported on passenger aircraft is screened, part of TSA's mission is ensuring the flow of commerce. Not transporting unscreened cargo could place the air cargo transportation industry at risk of experiencing economic disruptions, including shifts of cargo to other modes of transportation, which could negatively affect the air cargo business. In order to help ensure that it fulfills its mission and meets the 9/11 Commission Act mandate, TSA could benefit from identifying alternative measures in a contingency plan, should it become clear that the CCSP will not achieve the screening mandate while maintaining the flow of commerce.

TSA HAS MADE PROGRESS BUT FACES SEVERAL CHALLENGES AND LACKS A PLAN FOR ACHIEVING 100 PERCENT SCREENING OF INBOUND CARGO

TSA has made progress toward meeting the screening mandate as it applies to inbound cargo by taking steps to increase the percentage of inbound air cargo that has undergone screening. However, the agency faces several challenges in ensuring that 100 percent of inbound air cargo is screened, which will prevent it from meeting the mandate by the August 2010 deadline. While TSA is aware that it is unable to meet the screening mandate as it applies to inbound cargo, it has not yet determined when or how it will eventually meet the deadline.

TSA Has Taken Several Steps to Increase the Percentage of Inbound Cargo Being Screened

TSA has taken several steps to increase the percentage of inbound air cargo being screened. For example, TSA revised its requirements for foreign and U.S. air carrier security programs, effective May 1, 2010, to generally require air carriers to screen a certain percentage of shrink-wrapped and banded inbound cargo and 100 percent of inbound cargo that is not shrink-wrapped or banded.[66] According to our analysis of TSA information, shrink-wrapped and banded cargo makes up approximately 96 percent of inbound cargo, which means that a significant percentage of inbound air cargo is not required to be screened.[67] According to TSA, implementation of this requirement will result in the screening of 100 percent of inbound cargo transported on narrow-body aircraft since none of this cargo is shrink-wrapped or banded.[68]

Since TSA does not have the same regulatory reach to the supply chain in foreign countries as it does in the United States, it is taking a different approach to implementing the screening mandate as it applies to inbound cargo. This approach focuses on harmonizing its security standards with those of other nations.[69] For example, TSA is working with foreign governments to increase the amount of screened cargo, including working bilaterally with the European Commission (EC) and Canada, and quadrilaterally with the EC, Canada, and Australia. As part of these efforts, TSA recommended to the United Nations' International Civil Aviation Organization (ICAO) that the next revision of Annex 17 to the Convention of International Civil Aviation include an approach that would allow screening to take place at various points in the air cargo supply chain.[70]

According to TSA, ICAO's Aviation Security Panel met in March 2010 to finalize revisions to Annex 17, including TSA's proposed revision to add "screening" as a supply chain security concept. TSA has also supported the International Air Transport Association's (IATA) efforts to establish a secure supply chain approach to screening cargo for its member airlines and IATA's efforts to have these standards recognized internationally.[71]

In addition, TSA is working with CBP to leverage an existing CBP system, known as the Automated Targeting System (ATS), to identify and target elevated-risk inbound air cargo. ATS is a model that combines information from inbound cargo manifest lists and entry declaration information into shipment transactions and uses historical and other data to help target cargo shipments for inspection.[72] While CBP currently uses ATS to identify cargo for screening once it arrives in the United States, according to officials, TSA has established a TSA-CBP working group to focus on using ATS to target inbound air cargo for possible screening prior to departure from foreign locations. TSA and CBP officials stated that the working group met regularly since June 2009, though agency officials did not specify how frequently they met. As of February 2010, TSA and CBP officials stated that

TSA Has Made Progress but Faces Challenges... 117

they were conducting an exercise at Dulles International Airport for TSA to observe CBP's use of ATS, understand the full capabilities of ATS, and determine whether ATS can assist TSA's inbound air cargo screening efforts. TSA officials said that they were not in a position to provide time frames for completing the exercise since the effort is in the early stages. Should TSA determine that ATS is effective for targeting the screening of inbound air cargo, TSA plans for air carriers to conduct the screening of shipments identified as elevated risk prior to the cargo's transport to the United States. The air carriers will also be responsible for providing TSA with the results. In discussing how a system to target certain, elevated-risk shipments for screening will fit into TSA's overall plans to screen 100 percent of inbound air cargo, officials stated that ATS would provide an additional layer of scrutiny for all cargo entering the United States.[73]

To help assess the rigor and quality of foreign screening practices, TSA is also in the process of obtaining information from foreign countries on their respective air cargo screening levels and practices. According to officials, the agency has developed an assessment methodology in a question and answer format to collect information on each foreign country's air cargo security practices, and it has used the new methodology to collect initial information from one country. TSA has indicated that it will use the methodology to identify key security practices and that the information collected will also help determine if these practices are comparable to TSA requirements, which will provide TSA with details that can help determine how foreign standards align with TSA standards. TSA officials indicated that the methodology used to collect the information is part of a larger process that will involve collecting initial information, analyzing what was received, and submitting additional questions to the foreign countries. TSA anticipates storing the information gathered in a database, which it has not yet created. TSA officials were unable to provide time frames for use of the assessment methodology or completing the database because the effort is in the early stages.

TSA Faces Several Challenges in Meeting the Screening Mandate as It Applies to Inbound Cargo

While TSA has taken steps to increase the percentage of inbound cargo that has undergone screening, the agency faces several challenges in meeting the mandate. Consequently, TSA has stated that it will not be able to meet the screening mandate as it applies to inbound cargo. For example, in a March 4,

2010, hearing before the Subcommittee on Homeland Security, House Committee on Appropriations, in responding to questions, the Acting TSA Administrator stated that it could take several years before 100 percent of inbound cargo is screened. According to TSA screening inbound air cargo poses unique challenges, related, in part, to TSA's limited ability to regulate foreign entities. As such, TSA officials stated that the agency is focusing its air cargo screening efforts on domestic cargo and on screening elevated-risk inbound cargo as it works to address the challenges it faces in screening 100 percent of inbound cargo.

Inbound air cargo is currently being screened at lower levels than domestic air cargo. For example, while TSA removed almost all its screening exemptions for domestic cargo, TSA requirements continue to exempt from screening a significant amount of shrink-wrapped air cargo transported to the United States, which represents about 96 percent of all inbound cargo.[74] Effective May 1, 2010, TSA requires that a certain percentage of this cargo be screened. In April 2007, we reported that TSA's screening exemptions for inbound cargo could pose a risk to the air cargo supply chain and recommended that TSA assess whether these exemptions pose an unacceptable vulnerability and, if necessary, address these vulnerabilities. TSA agreed with our recommendation, but beyond expanding its requirement to screen 100 percent of inbound air cargo transported on narrow-body aircraft and a certain percentage of inbound cargo that is shrink-wrapped or placed on banded skids, has not yet reviewed, revised, or eliminated screening exemptions for cargo transported on inbound passenger flights, and did not provide a time frame for doing so.[75] We continue to believe that TSA should assess whether these exemptions pose an unacceptable security risk. TSA officials stated that once the modified ATS is in place, screening exemptions will be less relevant because air carriers will be more able to target the screening of elevated-risk cargo as an interim measure before 100 percent screening is achieved. However, the 9/11 Commission Act requires that all air cargo be physically screened and does not make exceptions for cargo that is not elevated risk.

TSA faces challenges in meeting the 100 percent screening mandate as it applies to inbound air cargo. For example, although TSA is authorized under U.S. law to ensure that all air carriers, foreign and domestic, operating to, from, or within the United States maintain the security measures included in their TSA-approved security programs and any applicable security directives or emergency amendments issued by TSA, this authority is limited.[76] Also, TSA has no legal jurisdiction over foreign nations. Specifically, TSA has been authorized by Congress to set standards for aviation security, including the authority to require that inbound cargo be screened before it departs for the United States. However, the agency also relies on foreign governments to implement and enforce—including conducting actual screening, in some cases—TSA's regulatory requirements.

Harmonizing TSA regulatory standards with those of foreign governments may be challenging because these efforts are voluntary and some foreign countries do not share the United States' concerns regarding air cargo security threats and risks. TSA officials caution that if TSA were to impose a strict cargo screening standard on all inbound cargo, many nations likely would be unable to meet such standards in the near term. This raises the prospect of reducing the flow of cargo on passenger aircraft. According to TSA, the effect of imposing such screening standards in the near future could result in increased costs for international passenger travel and for imported goods and possible reduction in passenger traffic and foreign imports. According to TSA officials, this could also undermine TSA's ongoing cooperative efforts to develop commensurate security systems with international partners. TSA's ongoing efforts to harmonize security standards with those of foreign nations are essential to achieving progress toward meeting the 100 percent screening mandate as it applies to inbound air cargo.

Identifying the precise level of screening being conducted on inbound air cargo is difficult because TSA lacks a mechanism to obtain actual data on all screening that is being conducted on inbound air cargo. TSA officials estimate that 55 percent of inbound cargo by weight is currently being screened and that 65 percent of inbound cargo by weight will be screened by August 2010.[77] However, these estimates are based on the current screening requirements of certain countries and are not based on actual data collected from air carriers or other entities, such as foreign governments, on what percentage of cargo is actually being screened.[78] For example, if a country requires that 100 percent of its cargo be screened, as the United Kingdom does, TSA counts all the cargo coming from that country as screened. While TSA officials stated that they discuss screening percentages with foreign government officials, the agency does not conduct any additional data verification to assess whether screening is conducted at, above, or below the required levels. In addition, because TSA's efforts to complete assessments of other countries' screening requirements are ongoing, the agency does not always know whether the screening requirements are consistent with TSA standards. The DHS Appropriations Act, 2009, requires TSA to report on the actual screening being conducted, by airport and air carrier.[79] To improve data collection efforts, as of May 2010, TSA requires air carriers to report on their actual screening levels for inbound air cargo, and TSA officials stated that an automated cargo reporting tool would be operational in May 2010 for this purpose. The May 2010 security program changes only require air carriers to report on the screening that they conduct and not on the screening conducted by other entities in the air cargo supply chain to meet the air cargo screening mandate. TSA officials stated that it may be challenging to obtain screening data from some foreign governments and other entities that conduct cargo screening. As such, TSA officials also stated that the agency may still use estimates, such as the current screening requirements of certain countries, when reporting data to Congress. Officials could not provide information on milestones or time frames for obtaining actual screening data for all inbound screening, including that conducted by air carriers and other entities in the air cargo supply chain, because the agency is still working to overcome inbound regulatory challenges. However, establishing time frames for implementing a plan is consistent with standard practices for program management.[80] Finalizing a plan to obtain actual screening data could help TSA obtain greater assurance that mandated screening levels are being met.

TSA Has Not Yet Determined How It Will Meet the Screening Mandate as It Applies to Inbound Cargo

TSA has not yet determined how it will meet the screening mandate as it applies to inbound air cargo. Although TSA has taken steps to increase the percentage of inbound cargo transported on passenger aircraft that is screened, the agency has not developed a plan, including milestones, for meeting the mandate as it applies to inbound cargo. While TSA officials have stated that the agency does not expect to meet the mandate as it applies to inbound cargo by the August 2010 deadline, TSA has not provided estimates of when the mandate will be met or when steps toward its achievement will be completed. Moreover, the steps that the agency is taking to enhance inbound air cargo security do not fully support the 100 percent cargo screening mandate. For example, TSA is focusing on developing its ability to utilize CBP's ATS to target elevated-risk cargo for screening. While we recognize this as a reasonable step to strengthen inbound air cargo security, TSA does not have a plan that articulates how this and other steps it is taking will fit together to achieve 100 percent screening.

The 9/11 Commission Act requires the establishment of a system to screen 100 percent of cargo transported on passenger aircraft, including inbound cargo. As we have reported in our prior work, a successful project plan— such as a plan that would be used to establish such a system—should consider all phases of the project and clearly state schedules and deadlines.[81] TSA reported that it is unable to identify a timeline for meeting the mandate for inbound cargo, stating that its efforts are long term, given the extensive work it must conduct with foreign governments and associations. However, interim milestones could help the agency provide reasonable assurance to Congress that it is taking steps to meet the mandate as it applies to inbound cargo. A plan that considers all phases of the project and clearly states schedules and deadlines could help position TSA to better measure progress it is making toward meeting the 9/11 Commission Act mandate as it relates to inbound air cargo and provide reasonable assurance that its efforts are implemented in a relatively timely manner.

CONCLUSIONS

Meeting the August 2010 mandate to establish a system to physically screen 100 percent of air cargo transported on passenger aircraft is a daunting task. In August 2010, unscreened cargo will not be allowed to fly on passenger aircraft, but leaving behind such cargo could affect the flow of commerce. Although the CCSP should help TSA meet the mandate as it applies to domestic cargo, addressing certain challenges could strengthen agency efforts and help ensure the CCSP's success. For example, TSA might benefit from developing a contingency plan should it become clear that participation levels are not sufficient to achieve the screening mandate without disruptions to the flow of commerce. Establishing milestones for completion of a staffing study to determine the number of inspectors needed to oversee CCSP participants could provide results that should better position TSA to obtain these inspection resources and help ensure that air carriers and CCSFs comply with TSA requirements. Moreover, the technology challenges TSA faces in screening cargo once it is loaded onto ULD pallets and containers highlight the need for a contingency plan in the event that industry stakeholders do not have the capacity to screen such air cargo. In addition, verifying industry-reported screening data could better position TSA in providing reasonable assurance that screening is being conducted at reported levels. Furthermore, developing a plan and milestones for screening in-transit cargo, which is not currently required to undergo physical screening, could help ensure that such cargo is screened in accordance with 9/11 Commission Act requirements and mitigate a risk to the air cargo transportation system. Developing a contingency plan that considers additional or alternative security measures will better position TSA to meet the mandate without disrupting the flow of commerce should it become clear that the challenges related to CCSP participation and screening technology will hinder the agency's efforts.

With regard to inbound air cargo, while TSA has taken some positive steps to increase the percentage of cargo that is screened, the agency could better address the challenges to screening this cargo. For example, finalizing its plans to obtain actual screening data for all inbound cargo screening, including time frames and milestones, could provide greater assurance that mandated screening levels are being met. In addition, determining how it will meet the screening mandate as it applies to inbound air cargo, including related milestones, could better position TSA in providing reasonable assurance that the agency is making progress toward meeting the screening mandate in a timely manner.

RECOMMENDATIONS FOR EXECUTIVE ACTION

To enhance efforts to secure the air cargo transportation system and establish a system to screen 100 percent of air cargo transported on passenger aircraft, we are recommending that the Administrator of TSA take the following five actions:

- Establish milestones for the completion of TSA's staffing study to assist in determining the resources necessary to provide CCSP oversight.
- Develop a mechanism to verify the accuracy of all screening data, both self-reported domestic data and inbound cargo data, through random checks or other practical means. For inbound air cargo, complete the agency's plan to obtain actual data, rather than estimates, for all inbound screening, including establishing time frames and milestones for completion of the plan.
- Develop a plan, with milestones, for how and when the agency intends to require the screening of in-transit cargo.
- Develop a contingency plan for meeting the mandate as it applies to domestic cargo that considers alternatives to address potential CCSP participation shortfalls and screening technology limitations.

- Develop a plan, with milestones, for how and when the agency intends to meet the mandate as it applies to inbound cargo.

AGENCY COMMENTS AND OUR EVALUATION

We provided a draft of our report to DHS and TSA on May 19, 2010, for review and comment. On June 23, 2010, DHS provided written comments from the department and TSA, which are reprinted in appendix I. In commenting on our report, TSA stated that it concurred with three recommendations, concurred in part with one recommendation, and did not concur with another recommendation. For the recommendations for which TSA concurred or concurred in part, the agency identified actions taken or planned to implement them. Although TSA concurred with part of our second recommendation, the actions TSA reported that the agency has taken do not fully address the intent of this recommendation.

Regarding our first recommendation that TSA establish milestones for the completion of its staffing study to assist in determining the resources necessary to provide CCSP oversight, TSA concurred. TSA stated that as part of the staffing study, the agency is working to develop a model to identify the number of required TSIs and that this effort would be completed in the fall of 2010. If this model includes an analysis of the resources needed to provide CCSP oversight under various scenarios, it will address the intent of our recommendation.

TSA concurred in part with our second recommendation that the agency develop a mechanism to verify the accuracy of domestic and inbound screening data, including obtaining actual data on all inbound screening. TSA concurred with the need to capture data for inbound cargo and stated that as of May 1, 2010, the agency issued changes to air carriers' standard security programs that require air carriers to report inbound cargo screening data to TSA. However, as noted in this report, these requirements apply to air carriers and the screening that they conduct and not to the screening conducted by other entities, such as foreign governments. Thus, TSA will continue to rely in part on estimates to report inbound cargo screening levels. We recognize that it may be challenging for TSA to obtain cargo screening data from foreign governments; however, the agency could require air carriers to report on cargo screening for all inbound cargo they transport, including the screening conducted by foreign governments or other entities. This would be similar to air carriers' domestic cargo screening reporting requirements which require air carriers to report on cargo that they screen as well as cargo screened by CCSFs. We continue to believe that it is important for TSA to obtain data for all screening conducted on inbound cargo so that it can provide assurance to Congress that this cargo is being screened in accordance with the 9/11 Commission Act screening mandate. TSA stated that verifying the accuracy of domestic screening data will continue to be a challenge because there is no means to cross-reference local screening logs—which include screening information on specific shipments—with screening reports submitted by air carriers to TSA that do not contain such information. We acknowledge TSA's potential challenges in cross-referencing screening logs with screening reports and have modified the report to reflect this challenge. However, as noted in this report, TSA could consider a quality review mechanism similar to the compliance measurement program used by CBP, which includes regular quality reviews to ensure accuracy in findings and management oversight to validate results. TSA could also develop another mechanism for verifying the accuracy of the screening data through random checks—other than those of the screening logs—or other practical means. Doing so would address the intent of our recommendation. Given that the agency uses these data to report to Congress its compliance with the screening mandate as it applies to domestic cargo, we continue to believe that verifying the accuracy of the screening data is important so that TSA will be better positioned to provide reasonable assurance that screening is being conducted at reported levels.

TSA concurred with our third recommendation that TSA develop a plan for how and when the agency intends to require the screening of in-transit cargo. TSA stated that the agency has implemented changes, effective August 1, 2010, that will require 100 percent of in-transit cargo to be screened unless it can otherwise be verified as screened. TSA's action is an important step toward addressing the potential security vulnerability associated with in-transit cargo and if implemented effectively, will address the intent of our recommendation. Because this is a significant change and potentially operationally challenging, it will be important to closely monitor the industry's understanding and implementation of this requirement to help ensure that 100 percent screening of in-transit cargo is being conducted.

TSA did not concur with our fourth recommendation to develop a contingency plan for meeting the mandate as it applies to domestic cargo that considers alternatives to address potential CCSP participation shortfalls and screening technology limitations. TSA stated that a contingency plan is unnecessary since effective August 1, 2010, 100 percent of domestic cargo transported on passenger aircraft will be required to be screened. The agency also stated that there is no feasible contingency plan that can be implemented by TSA that does not compromise security or create disparities in the availability of screening resources. However, the agency noted that several alternatives are available to and are currently being exercised by industry. The agency also stated that TSA developed the CCSP in collaboration with industry stakeholders to alleviate the burden on airlines to screen 100 percent of cargo while still meeting the mandate. We disagree that a contingency plan is unnecessary and unfeasible. As noted in this report, although TSA's approach would ensure that 100 percent of domestic cargo transported on passenger aircraft is screened, not transporting unscreened cargo could negatively affect the flow of commerce. In addition, while we recognize the CCSP as a positive and critical step toward achieving the screening mandate as it applies to domestic cargo, we continue to believe that there are feasible alternatives that TSA should consider to address potential CCSP participation shortfalls and screening technology limitations. Such alternatives discussed in this report include mandating CCSP participation for certain members of the air cargo supply chain and requiring the screening of some or all cargo before it is loaded onto ULD pallets and containers. Effective May 1, 2010, TSA embraced one of the alternatives cited in this report by requiring freight forwarder CCSFs to screen all cargo before it is loaded onto ULD pallets and containers. Expanding this requirement to additional industry stakeholders could be a feasible alternative to address both CCSP participation shortfalls and screening technology limitations. Moreover, although many industry stakeholders may support the CCSP, key partners in the program—shippers—have not joined the program at the levels targeted by TSA, thus jeopardizing its success. Therefore, we continue to believe that it is prudent that TSA consider developing a contingency plan for meeting the air cargo screening mandate without disrupting the flow of commerce.

Finally, in regard to our fifth recommendation that TSA develop a plan for how and when the agency intends to meet the mandate as it applies to inbound cargo, TSA concurred and stated that TSA is drafting milestones as part of a plan that will generally require air carriers to conduct 100 percent screening by a specific date. If implemented effectively, this plan will address the intent of our recommendation.

In addition, DHS noted in its written comments that CCSFs have reported to TSA that they have the capacity to screen nearly the entire remaining unscreened cargo volume and that air carriers have reported to TSA that they do not anticipate any major disruptions to the transport of air cargo on August 2010. We were not able to verify these assertions because TSA did not provide supporting documentation. It is also important to note that having the potential capacity to screen air cargo does not ensure that this screening will take place when the 100 percent screening mandate goes into effect in August 2010.

TSA also provided us with technical comments, which we considered and incorporated in the report where appropriate.

APPENDIX I. COMMENTS FROM THE DEPARTMENT OF HOMELAND SECURITY

U.S. Department of Homeland Security
Washington, DC 20528

June 22, 2010

Mr. Steve Lord
Director, Homeland Security & Justice Issues
U.S. Government Accountability Office (GAO)
441 G Street, NW
Washington, DC 20548

Dear Mr. Lord:

Thank you for the opportunity to review and comment on GAO 10-446, the draft report titled: *Aviation Security: TSA Has Made Progress But Faces Challenges in Meeting the Statutory Mandate for Screening Air Cargo on Passenger Aircraft*. The Transportation Security Administration (TSA) appreciates the professionalism demonstrated by GAO's team members in conducting this difficult and broad-ranging review. TSA also values the investigative panel's review of this agency's efforts to enable the air cargo industry to achieve the 100 percent air cargo screening mandate of the Implementing Recommendations of the 9/11 Commission Act (9/11 Act).

Since August 2007, when TSA was tasked with establishing a system to screen 100 percent of cargo transported on passenger aircraft, we have implemented a major new security program called the Certified Cargo Screening Program (CCSP), issued regulations and security program amendments to incrementally increase the level of screening of cargo transported on passenger aircraft departing U.S. locations, engaged in a broad-based campaign to educate industry on the 100 percent screening requirement and the benefits of CCSP participation, and significantly increased the number and types of technologies approved for screening air cargo to support the screening mandate.

TSA has certified over 720 entities as Certified Cargo Screening Facilities (CCSFs) since the CCSP was initiated as a pilot program in 2008. These entities currently are screening more than 40 percent of the cargo, by weight, carried on passenger aircraft departing U.S. airports. They have reported to TSA that they have the capacity to screen nearly the entire remaining unscreened volume as we approach the August 2010 deadline. Additionally, air carriers are continuing to invest in screening equipment, and have also reported that they do not anticipate any major disruptions.

In October 2008, TSA began increasing the level of screening required on cargo transported on passenger aircraft in the United States by establishing a requirement to screen 100 percent of cargo transported on narrow body aircraft. This measure fully protects 96 percent of all domestic passenger aircraft flights, which carry more than 86

percent of all aircraft passengers in the United States. Subsequent updates to TSA security programs required 50 percent screening by February 1, 2009, and most recently, 75 percent screening by May 1, 2010. Both levels have been successfully met by industry.

- 2 -

TSA has reached out to more than 100,000 entities on the 100 percent screening requirement and the CCSP, working largely through major industry associations to engage stakeholders through webinars, conferences, newsletters, articles and advertisements in trade journals and the popular press.

When the 9/11 Act was passed, no equipment had been tested or approved specifically for cargo screening. TSA has since created an approved technologies list that contains more than 50 technologies, including Advanced Technology (AT) X-ray capable of screening large cargo configurations, as well as Explosives Trace Detection (ETD), Explosive Detection Systems (EDS), and most recently Electromagnetic Devices (EMD).

While industry has not yet achieved 100 percent screening for international inbound cargo due to the challenges of implementing a supply chain screening program internationally, TSA intends to require an increased level of screening for international inbound cargo as we continue to facilitate industry's achievement of 100 percent screening in the next few years. A combination of incremental increases in the screening requirements for carriers as well as recognition of foreign national cargo security programs, are key components of that strategy.

TSA appreciates the work of GAO in its review of TSA Air Cargo Programs, and we will continue to address the issues identified by GAO. Our continued progress demonstrates our commitment to TSA's mission of securing our Nation's transportation systems and ensuring the freedom of movement of people and commerce. TSA's specific responses to GAO's recommendations are below.

Recommendation 1: Establish milestones for the completion of TSA's staffing study.

TSA concurs. As part of the Transportation Security Inspector (TSI) study, TSA is working to develop a demand model to be used to identify the number of TSIs needed at a particular location based on various factors, to include the number of regulated entities, such as CCSFs. This is expected to be completed in the Fall of 2010. TSA has already established an interim model that determines a ratio of inspectors to entities and that also considers other factors, such as cargo volume. TSA has already used the interim model in order to develop a plan for deployment of 50 TSI-Cargo (TSI-C) in fiscal year 2010.

Recommendation 2: Develop a mechanism to verify the accuracy of all screening data, both self-reported domestic data and inbound cargo data, through random checks or other practical means. For inbound cargo data, complete the agency's

plan to obtain actual data, rather than estimates, on all inbound screening, including establishing timeframes and milestones for completion of the plan.

TSA concurs in part. TSA concurs with the need to capture data for inbound cargo and as of May 1, 2010, TSA issued changes to the standard security programs that require this data to be reported to TSA. However, the ability to verify the accuracy of screening data provided by regulated parties will continue to be a challenge. While TSI-C's can obtain specific screening logs for screening activity, there is currently no means to cross-reference local screening logs (which provide information as to how and by whom a particular shipment was screened) with carrier-level reports. Carrier reports themselves are a compilation of statistics provided by multiple locations. No specific shipment numbers are required as part of this process, and to add such a requirement would be a significant

- 3 -

burden to industry. TSA will verify the accuracy of this data through random checks and inspections of screening logs.

Recommendation 3: Develop a plan, with milestones, for how and when the agency intends to require the screening of in-transit cargo.

TSA concurs. TSA has already taken significant steps to accomplish this objective, and has implemented changes to the Foreign Air Carrier Model Security Program and the U.S. Aircraft Operator Standard Security Program; effective August 1, 2010, 100 percent of all cargo transported on passenger aircraft from U.S. airports will be required to be screened.

Recommendation 4: Develop a contingency plan for meeting the mandate as it applies to domestic cargo that considers alternatives to address potential CCSP participation shortfalls and screening technology limitations.

TSA does not concur. Effective August 1, 2010, 100 percent of all cargo transported on passenger aircraft from U.S. airports will be required to be screened; to develop a contingency plan that suggests otherwise is unnecessary. TSA contends that there is no feasible contingency plan that can be implemented by TSA that does not compromise security or create disparities in the availability of screening resources among airports and/or commodity sectors. However, based on each entity's business model, there are alternatives that an entity can use including earlier shipment delivery times by air carriers for unscreened cargo, as well as the use of all cargo aircraft or surface alternatives. TSA has developed the CCSP in collaboration with industry stakeholders to alleviate the burden on airlines to screen 100 percent of cargo while still meeting this mandate. Industry supports this decision to screen cargo earlier in the supply chain before reaching the airlines.

Recommendation 5: Develop a plan, with milestones, for how and when the agency intends to meet the mandate as it applies to inbound cargo.

TSA concurs. TSA is drafting a set of milestones that will require all carriers to attain 100 percent screening by a specific date, unless other national cargo security programs are submitted, reviewed, and accepted as providing commensurate levels of security. We will be happy to share this plan with GAO when it is completed.

Sincerely yours,

Jerald E. Levine
Director
Departmental GAO/OIG Liaison Office

APPENDIX II. ACKNOWLEDGMENTS

In addition to the contact named above, Steve D. Morris, Assistant Director, and Rebecca Kuhlmann Taylor, Analyst-in-Charge, managed this review. Scott M. Behen, Erin C. Henderson, Elke Kolodinski, Linda S. Miller, Matthew Pahl, and Yanina Golburt Samuels made significant contributions to the work. David K. Hooper and Thomas Lombardi provided legal support. Stanley J. Kostyla assisted with design and methodology. Pille Anvelt and Tina Cheng helped develop the report's graphics. John W. Cooney, Elizabeth C. Dunn, Richard B. Hung, Brendan Kretzschmar, and Amelia B. Shachoy also provided support.

End Notes

[1] For the purposes of this report, domestic cargo refers to cargo transported by air within the United States and from the United States to a foreign location by both U.S. and foreign air carriers, and inbound cargo refers to cargo transported by both U.S. and foreign air carriers from a foreign location to the United States. These cargo statistics were provided by the Transportation Security Administration from the Bureau of Transportation Statistics.

[2] Specific threat details are classified and are not discussed in this report. Generally, the threat that has been identified by TSA is that of an improvised explosive device.

[3] Pub. L. No. 107-71, 115 Stat. 597 (2001).

[4] CBP has primary responsibility for preventing terrorists and implements of terrorism from entering the United States.

[5] Pub. L. No. 110-53, § 1602, 121 Stat. 266, 477-80 (codified at 49 U.S.C. § 44901(g)).

[6] See 49 U.S.C. § 44901(g)(5). For the purposes of this report, physical screenin is generally used to describe screening for purposes of the air cargo screening mandate.

[7] The policies and procedures we reviewed include Aircraft Operator Standard Security Program, Change 5A, February 26, 2009; Aircraft Operator Standard Security Program, Change 9, April 1, 2010; Aircraft Operator Standard Security Program, Change 9A, June 3, 2010; Alternate Procedure to Indirect Air Carrier Standard Security Program (AP-IACSSP-08-002-C), February 25, 2009; Alternate Procedure to Indirect Air Carrier Standard Security Program (AP-IACSSP-08-001-E), February 25, 2009; Alternate Procedure to Indirect Air Carrier Standard Security Program (AP-IACSSP-08-002-E), April 19, 2010; Certified Cargo Screening Program Order, Change 2, February 26, 2009; Foreign Air Carrier Model Security Program, Change 8A, February 26, 2009; Foreign Air Carrier Model Security Program, Change 12, April 1, 2010; Foreign Air Carrier Model Security Program, Change 12A, June 3, 2010; and Indirect Air Carrier Standard Security Program, Change 3A, February 26, 2009.

[8] There are about 450 commercial airports in the United States. TSA classifies airports into one of five categories (X, I, II, III, and IV) based on various factors, such as the total number of takeoffs and landings annually, the extent to which passengers are screened at the airport,

and other special security considerations. In general, category X airports have the largest number of passenger boardings, and category IV airports have the smallest.

[9] For the purposes of this report, the term freight forwarder only includes those freight forwarders that are regulated by TSA, also referred to as indirect air carriers. A freight forwarder is a company that consolidates cargo from multiple shippers onto a master air waybill—a manifest of the consolidated shipment—and delivers the shipment to air carriers for transport.

[10] The associations whose officials we interviewed include one air carrier association that represents 16 of the principal U.S. air carriers and their affiliates, which transport more than 90 percent of U.S. air carrier passenger and cargo traffic; one air carrier association that represents about 230 U.S. and foreign air carriers that account for 93 percent of scheduled international air traffic; one air carrier association that represents 16 small U.S. air carriers, many of which fly all-cargo and charter aircraft; one freight forwarder association that represents 330 companies and about 3,000 offices out of approximately 4,500 domestic freight forwarders, and a variety of small, medium, and large domestic freight forwarders; one airport association whose commercial airport members represent more than 95 percent of domestic air carrier passenger and air cargo traffic in North America; and one pilots' association that represents 28,000 out of 90,000 pilots at U.S. air carriers.

[11] GAO, *2010 Census: Cost and Design Issues Need to Be Addressed Soon*, GAO-04-37 (Washington, D.C.: Jan. 15, 2004). This report reviewed a number of guides to project management and business process reengineering to help determine the key elements for successful project planning. The guides include Project Management Institute Standards Committee, *A Guide to the Project Management Body of Knowledge* © (1996); Information Technology Resource Board, *Project Management for Mission Critical Systems: A Handbook for Government Executives* (Apr. 5, 2001); Carnegie Mellon Software Engineering Institute, *Capability Maturity Model Integration Project Planning Guide* (March 2001); and GAO, *Business Process Reengineering Assessment Guide*, Version 3, GAO/AIMD-10.1.15 (Washington, D.C.: May 1997). See The Project Management Institute, *The Standard for Program Management* © (2006).

[12] Office of Management and Budget, *Guidelines for Ensuring and Maximizing the Quality, Objectivity, Utility, and Integrity of Information Disseminated by Federal Agencies* (October 2001).

[13] GAO-04-37.

[14] GAO, *Federal Law Enforcement Training Center: Capacity Planning and Management Oversight Need Improvement*, GAO-03-736 (Washington, D.C.: July 24, 2003).

[15] The six air cargo industry associations are those discussed earlier in this report.

[16] The Project Management Institute, *The Standard for Program Management*.

[17] GAO-04-37.

[18] All-cargo aircraft are aircraft that transport only cargo.

[19] These cargo statistics were provided by TSA from the Bureau of Transportation Statistics.

[20] H.R. Conf. Rep. No. 111-298, at 79 (2009). In fiscal year 2009, TSA allocated 85 proprietary canine teams—teams that are owned and operated full-time by TSA staff. TSA also has agreements with local law enforcement agencies, such as local police departments, for some of their canine teams to operate part-time in the air cargo environment. The transfer of 35 local law enforcement teams to TSA would increase the number of allocated TSA proprietary canine teams to 120. TSA tests technologies in laboratory and operational environments, evaluates the performance and effectiveness of technology against preset

standards, and upon successful completion of the assessments, deploys the technology at airports and air cargo facilities.

[21] A weapon of mass destruction could include nuclear, biological, chemical, or radiological devices.

[22] See 49 U.S.C. § 44901(g)(5). EDS uses computer-aided tomography X-rays to examine objects inside baggage and identify the characteristic signatures of threat explosives. ETD requires human operators to collect samples of items to be screened with swabs, which are chemically analyzed to identify any traces of explosive material. Certified explosives detection canine teams have been evaluated by TSA and shown to effectively detect explosive devices. Physical search together with manifest verification entails comparisons between air waybills and cargo contents to ensure that the contents of the cargo shipment match the cargo identified in documents filed by the shipper.

[23] TSA exempts some categories of air cargo from physical screening and requires alternative methods of screening, such as verifying shipper and cargo information and visually inspecting the cargo shipment, rather than opening the shipment and physically searching its contents or screening it with technology. TSA determines whether domestic cargo is subject to alternative methods of screening based on professional judgment and the results of the air cargo vulnerability assessments. For the purposes of this report, the phrase "exempt cargo" and the word "exemption" refer to cargo that is subject to such alternative screening measures. Narrow-body aircraft, such as Boeing 737s and Airbus 320s, are defined by fuselage diameter, and most narrow-body aircraft have only one aisle. Narrow-body aircraft that fly in the United States do not carry ULDs that allow packages to be consolidated in a container or pallet. Wide-body aircraft are also defined by fuselage diameter and can carry ULDs.

[24] According to statistics provided by TSA from the Bureau of Transportation Statistics, narrow-body aircraft make up 97 percent of passenger flights and transport more than 90 percent of passengers traveling on domestic passenger flights.

[25] Details on TSA's screening exemptions are Sensitive Security Information and are not discussed in this report.

[26] 49 C.F.R. §§ 1544.205(g)(1)(ii), 1546.205(g)(1)(ii).

[27] The agency issued an interim order in December 2008 to allow shippers and other entities that were previously not regulated by TSA to screen, accept, and transfer air cargo.

[28] 74 Fed. Reg. 47672, September 16, 2009.

[29] A security threat assessment is a check of personnel against intelligence records and databases, including terrorist watch lists, and a limited immigration check, to verify that they do not pose a security threat.

[30] Beginning in August 2010, at the 100 percent screening deadline, TSA officials told us that freight forwarder CCSFs will also be required to screen 100 percent of cargo being delivered to wide-body aircraft.

[31] TSA refers to CCSP outreach coordinators as principal cargo security analysts.

[32] Under the IFR, TSA plans to engage TSA-approved third-party firms to validate and certify CCSP applicants. TSA refers to these third-party validators as third-party assessment validation firms. According to TSA officials, CCSP outreach coordinators plan to manage the oversight and certification of the third-party validators.

[33] The other industry association officials with whom we spoke did not comment on this issue.

[34] GAO, *Aviation Security: Preliminary Observations on TSA's Progress and Challenges in Meeting the Statutory Mandate for Screening Air Cargo on Passenger Aircraft,* GAO-09-422T (Washington, D.C.: Mar. 18, 2009).

[35] Initially, the Air Cargo Screening Technology Pilot, or the Indirect Air Carrier technology pilot as it is named in the IFR, was limited to high-volume freight forwarders (i.e., freight forwarders processing at least 200 shipments annually per location that contain cargo consolidated from multiple shippers). However, in November 2008, TSA issued a second announcement seeking additional high-volume freight forwarders and independent cargo screening facilities to apply for the pilot. Moreover, entities that do not participate in the pilot will not receive TSA funding to purchase screening technology.

[36] In December 2009, TSA extended the expiration date of the approved technologies to January 2012. For the purposes of this report, when discussing TSA's approved or qualified technology lists, X-ray refers to X-ray, advanced technology X-ray, or both.

[37] The qualification process will also test future technologies not currently on the approved list once they mature and become approved.

[38] TSA canine teams conduct primary and secondary screening of cargo. Primary screening counts toward meeting the air cargo screening mandate. Secondary screening provides spot checks of the screening already conducted by air carriers and CCSFs. TSA could not provide a breakdown of the 145 million pounds of cargo between primary and secondary screening. Based on 2008 cargo totals, 145 million pounds of cargo represents about 3 percent of domestic air cargo.

[39] In fiscal year 2010, TSA projects a total of 805 canine teams in aviation, mass transit, and maritime systems. In the fiscal year 2011 budget justification, TSA is requesting funding for an additional 275 explosives detection canine teams to operate in the area of aviation security.

[40] The DHS Appropriations Act, 2009, requires TSA to report to the House and Senate Appropriations Committees quarterly on the actual screening conducted, by airport and air carrier. See Pub. L. No. 110-329, § 515(d), 122 Stat. 3574, 3683.

[41] Through an agreement with the House and Senate Appropriations Committees, TSA did not provide a 1st Quarter report.

[42] Details on TSA's covert testing program are Sensitive Security Information and are not discussed in this report.

[43] The CCSP allows air cargo industry stakeholders, such as an air cargo handling agent, to establish independent cargo screening facilities to provide screening services for shippers or freight forwarders that have not joined the program and do not want the air carriers to screen their cargo. These independent facilities screen cargo for a fee, according to CCSP guidelines. For the purposes of this report, we refer to independent cargo screening facilities as independent CCSFs.

[44] The screening percentages in fig. 4 have been rounded to the nearest percentage point. However, the actual percentages for March 2010 sum to 68 percent.

[45] According to TSA, as of March 2010, the agency had certified 397 freight forwarder CCSFs, 143 shipper CCSFs, and 43 independent CCSFs out of an estimated population of 4,500 freight forwarders at 12,000 locations and 15,000 shippers at 2 million locations.

[46] A freight forwarder's size is determined by its annual sales. For example, a freight forwarder with $5 million or less in annual sales is considered to be small.

[47] TSA's Regulatory Activities Plan establishes the minimum number of inspections, depending on airport size and other factors, TSIs are to conduct for each type of regulated entity.

[48] During the 90-day nonenforcement period following certification—during which CCSFs are not required to screen at mandated levels while they are developing their screening systems—TSA field offices may also require TSIs to visit CCSFs in their areas of responsibility to provide guidance on the TSA screening requirements that the entities must

TSA Has Made Progress but Faces Challenges... 133

implement. TSA field offices are to schedule comprehensive inspections after the 90-day period expires.

[49] According to TSA data, inspectors conducted 553 comprehensive inspections of CCSFs from February 1, 2009, through February 22, 2010, as the program was developing. Therefore, in the next year, inspectors will need to at least double their comprehensive inspections of CCSFs to reach the 1,166 target. Additional CCSFs and extra comprehensive inspections will further affect this increase.

[50] We analyzed inspection data from February 1, 2009, through February 22, 2010. As of February 22, 2010, TSIs had performed inspections on 68 percent (392 of 576) of all certified CCSFs and approximately 77 percent (392 of 508) of those eligible for inspection that were beyond the 90-day nonenforcement period. We also calculated that as of February 22, 2010, 146 CCSFs had received two annual inspections. Because CCSFs are not eligible for inspection within 90 days of certification, and some CCSFs had been certified for less than 6 months and had not had their second required annual inspections, we calculated that 445 CCSFs were enrolled approximately 6 months prior to February 22, 2010, and at least 285 CCSFs were enrolled 9 months prior to February 22, 2010.

[51] Details on the number and type of CCSF compliance inspection violations are Sensitive Security Information and are not discussed in this report.

[52] GAO-04-37.

[53] The Project Management Institute, *The Standard for Program Management*.

[54] Cargo may be screened before it is loaded onto ULD pallets or containers.

[55] According to TSA officials, these other S&T Directorate reports include *Test and Evaluation Report for Trace Explosives Detection for Cargo Screening* of September 2008, and *Comparative Report of Eight Explosive Trace Detection Systems in Particle Mode for Cargo Screening* of September 2009.

[56] See GAO, *Defense Acquisitions: Measuring the Value of DOD's Weapon Programs Requires Starting with Realistic Baselines*, GAO-09-543T (Washington, D.C.: Apr. 1, 2009). For an additional example of such programs, see GAO, *Secure Border Initiative: DHS Has Faced Challenges Deploying Technology and Fencing Along the Southwest Border*, GAO-10-651T (Washington, D.C.: May 4, 2010).

[57] See GAO, *Aviation Security: DHS and TSA Have Researched, Developed, and Begun Deploying Passenger Checkpoint Screening Technologies, but Continue to Face Challenges*, GAO-10-128 (Washington, D.C.: Oct. 7, 2009).

[58] Department of Homeland Security, Office of Inspector General, *Security of Air Cargo During Ground Transportation*, OIG-10-09 (Washington, D.C., November 2009).

[59] We used the industry-reported data in fig. 4 of this report because we found them to be sufficiently reliable to provide a general indication of cargo screening levels. However, as discussed here, questions exist about the accuracy of the industry-reported data.

[60] Office of Management and Budget, *Guidelines for Ensuring and Maximizing the Quality, Objectivity, Utility, and Integrity of Information Disseminated by Federal Agencies*.

[61] Details on TSA's screening exemptions are Sensitive Security Information and are not discussed in this report.

[62] Details on TSA's approved screening methods are Sensitive Security Information and are not discussed in this report.

[63] TSA requirements to screen inbound cargo will be discussed in further detail in a later section of this report. Details on TSA's screening exemptions are Sensitive Security Information and are not discussed in this report. For additional information on the issue of screening

exemptions, see GAO, *Review of the Transportation Security Administration's Air Cargo Screening Exemptions Report,* GAO-08-1055R (Washington, D.C.: Aug. 15, 2008).

[64] GAO-04-37.

[65] GAO-03-736.

[66] Details on TSA's screening requirements are Sensitive Security Information and are not discussed in this report. Prior to May 1, 2010, TSA generally required air carriers to screen 50 percent of nonexempt inbound cargo transported on passenger aircraft and a certain percentage of all inbound cargo transported on passenger aircraft.

[67] Banded cargo is cargo with heavy-duty metal, plastic, or nylon bands that secure all sides of the cargo shipment or secure the cargo shipment to a skid. While TSA officials could not provide a precise estimate of what percentage of inbound cargo this shrink-wrapped or banded cargo represents, about 96 percent of inbound cargo arrives in the United States on wide-body aircraft—the vast majority of which is transported on shrink-wrapped or banded skids.

[68] According to statistics provided by TSA from the Bureau of Transportation Statistics, in 2008, narrow-body flights made up 69 percent of inbound flights and transported 45 percent of inbound passengers.

[69] TSA does not regulate foreign freight forwarders, or individuals or businesses that have their cargo shipped by air to the United States. The term harmonization is used to describe countries' efforts to coordinate their security practices to enhance security and increase efficiency by avoiding duplication of effort. Harmonization efforts can include countries mutually recognizing and accepting each other's existing practices—which could represent somewhat different approaches to achieve the same outcome—as well as working to develop mutually acceptable uniform standards.

[70] ICAO is a specialized agency of the United Nations with the primary objective to provide for the safe, orderly, and efficient development of international civil aviation.

[71] IATA is an industry association that represents about 230 air carriers constituting 93 percent of international scheduled air traffic. IATA's approach, called Secure Freight, is an attempt to create an air cargo industry comprising certified secure operators in secure supply chains operating to international cargo security standards recognized by relevant state authorities. A pilot of the Secure Freight program is scheduled to begin in the first half of 2010.

[72] Air carriers departing from any foreign location in the Americas, including Mexico, Central America, and areas of South America north of the equator, must submit manifest information to CBP no later than the time of flight departure (the time at which wheels are up on the aircraft and the aircraft is en route directly to the United States). In the case of air carriers departing from any other foreign location, CBP requires that manifest information be submitted 4 hours prior to the flight's arrival in the United States. Unlike TSA's planned efforts to screen cargo prior to departure, CBP screens cargo once it enters the United States.

[73] We have previously reported on TSA and CBP efforts regarding securing inbound cargo and recommended that the agencies improve coordination and information sharing. TSA and CBP's collaboration on ATS is a response to this recommendation. In addition, CBP created the International Air Cargo Strategic Plan in June 2007 to assist the agency in increasing aviation security related to inbound air cargo. For more information, see GAO, *Aviation Security: Federal Efforts to Secure U.S.-Bound Air Cargo Are in the Early Stages and Could Be Strengthened,* GAO-07-660 (Washington, D.C.: Apr. 30, 2007).

[74] Details on TSA's screening requirements and exemptions are Sensitive Security Information and are not discussed in this report.

[75] GAO-07-660.

[76] See 49 U.S.C. §§ 44903, 44906; see also 49 C.F.R. §§ 1544.3, 1546.3. Although TSA security requirements follow the ICAO standards and recommended practices, TSA may subject air carriers operating to, from, or within the United States to any requirements necessary and assess compliance with such requirements, as the interests of aviation and national security dictate. See 49 U.S.C. § 44906.

[77] This includes both exempt and nonexempt cargo, under TSA's definitions. Since the screening of inbound cargo is conducted based on the standards of each individual country, it may not be conducted in accordance with TSA standards. For example, at least one country allows the use of large X-ray machines to inspect entire pallets of cargo that will be transported on passenger aircraft, without requiring the pallets to be broken down. In addition, two European countries use canines in a different manner than TSA to inspect air cargo for explosives. Specifically, these countries are using the Remote Air Sampling for Canine Olfaction technique, which involves the use of highly trained dogs to sniff air samples collected from air cargo or trucks through a specially designed filter. Such screening standards may produce different results from TSA's screening standards. See GAO-07-660 for more details.

[78] According to TSA officials, the agency does not know the screening requirements for every country that transports air cargo into the United States. TSA assumes that other countries are in compliance, at a minimum, with TSA's regulation that a certain percentage of inbound air cargo be screened.

[79] Pub. L. No. 110-329, § 515(d), 122 Stat. 3574, 3683.

[80] The Project Management Institute, *The Standard for Program Management*.

[81] GAO-04-37.

In: Air Cargo Security
Editor: Pierre Turrión

ISBN: 978-1-62100-054-9
© 2012 Nova Science Publishers, Inc.

Chapter 4

TESTIMONY BEFORE THE SUBCOMMITTEE ON TRANSPORTATION SECURITY, COMMITTEE ON HOMELAND SECURITY, HOUSE OF REPRESENTATIVES

AVIATION SECURITY: PROGRESS MADE, BUT CHALLENGES PERSIST IN MEETING THE SCREENING MANDATE FOR AIR CARGO[*]

United States Government Accountability Office

WHY GAO DID THIS STUDY

The Department of Homeland Security's (DHS) Transportation Security Administration (TSA) is the federal agency with primary responsibility for securing the air cargo system. The Implementing Recommendations of the 9/11 Commission Act of 2007 mandated DHS to establish a system to screen 100 percent of cargo flown on passenger aircraft by August 2010. GAO

---

[*] This is an edited, reformatted and augmented version of the United States Government Accountability Office publication GAO-11-413T, dated March 9, 2011.

reviewed TSA's progress in meeting the act's screening mandate, and any related challenges it faces for both domestic (cargo transported within and from the United States) and inbound cargo (cargo bound for the United States). This statement is based on prior reports and testimonies issued from April 2007 through December 2010 addressing the security of the air cargo transportation system and selected updates made in February and March 2011. For the updates, GAO obtained information on TSA's air cargo security programs and interviewed TSA officials.

WHAT GAO RECOMMENDS

GAO has made recommendations in prior work to strengthen air cargo screening. Although not fully concurring with all recommendations, TSA has taken or has a number of actions underway to address them. Continued attention is needed to ensure some recommendations are addressed, such as establishing a mechanism to verify screening data. TSA provided technical comments on the information in this statement, which GAO incorporated as appropriate.

WHAT GAO FOUND

As of August 2010, TSA reported that it met the mandate to screen 100 percent of air cargo as it applies to domestic cargo, but as GAO reported in June 2010, TSA lacked a mechanism to verify the accuracy of the data used to make this determination. TSA took several actions in meeting this mandate for domestic cargo, including creating a voluntary program to facilitate screening throughout the air cargo supply chain; taking steps to test technologies for screening air cargo; and expanding its explosives detection canine program, among other things. However, in June 2010 GAO reported that TSA did not have a mechanism to verify screening data and recommended that TSA establish such a mechanism. TSA partially concurred with this recommendation and stated that verifying such data would be challenging. As GAO reported in June 2010, data verification is important to provide reasonable assurance that screening is being conducted at reported levels. As GAO further reported in June 2010, there is no technology approved or qualified by TSA to screen cargo once it is loaded onto a pallet or container—

both of which are common means of transporting domestic air cargo on passenger aircraft. As a result, questions remain about air carriers' ability to effectively screen air cargo on such aircraft.

TSA has also taken a number of steps to enhance the security of inbound air cargo, but also faces challenges that could hinder its ability to meet the screening mandate. TSA moved its deadline for meeting the 100 percent screening mandate as it applies to inbound air cargo to the end of 2011, up 2 years from when the TSA administrator previously reported the agency would meet this mandate. According to TSA officials, the agency determined it was feasible to accelerate the deadline as a result of trends in air carrier reported screening data and discussions with air cargo industry leaders regarding progress made by industry to secure cargo on passenger aircraft. TSA also took steps to enhance the security of inbound cargo following the October 2010 Yemen air cargo bomb attempt—such as requiring additional screening of high-risk cargo prior to transport on an all-cargo aircraft. However, TSA continues to face challenges GAO identified in June 2010 that could impact TSA's ability to meet this screening mandate as it applies to inbound air cargo. For example, GAO reported that TSA's screening percentages were estimates and were not based on actual data collected from air carriers or other entities, such as foreign governments, and recommended that TSA establish a mechanism to verify the accuracy of these data. TSA partially agreed, and required air carriers to report inbound cargo screening data effective May 2010. However, TSA officials stated while current screening percentages are based on actual data reported by air carriers, verifying the accuracy of the screening data is difficult. It is important for TSA to have complete and accurate data to verify that the agency can meet the screening mandate. GAO will continue to monitor these issues as part of its ongoing review of TSA's efforts to secure inbound air cargo, the final results to be issued later this year.

Mr. Chairman and Members of the Subcommittee:

I appreciate the opportunity to participate in today's hearing to discuss the security of the nation's air cargo system. In 2009, about 6.5 billion pounds of cargo were transported on U.S. passenger flights—approximately 56 percent of which was transported domestically (domestic cargo) and 44 percent of which was transported on flights arriving in the United States from a foreign location (inbound cargo).[1] The October 2010 discovery of explosive devices in air cargo packages bound for the United States from Yemen, and the 2009 Christmas Day plot to detonate an explosive device during an international flight bound for Detroit, provide vivid reminders that civil aviation remains a key terrorist target. According to the Transportation Security Administration

(TSA), the security threat posed by terrorists introducing explosive devices in air cargo shipments is significant, and the risk and likelihood of such an attack directed at passenger aircraft is high.

The Aviation and Transportation Security Act (ATSA), enacted into law shortly after the September 11, 2001, terrorist attacks, established TSA and gave the agency responsibility for securing all modes of transportation, including the nation's civil aviation system, which includes air carrier operations (domestic and foreign) to, from, and within the United States.[2] For example, ATSA requires that TSA provide for the screening of all passengers and property, including cargo, transported on passenger aircraft.[3] ATSA further requires that a system be in operation, as soon as practicable after ATSA's enactment (on November 19, 2001), to screen, inspect, or otherwise ensure the security of the cargo transported by all-cargo aircraft—generally, aircraft that carry only cargo and no passengers—to, from, and within the United States.[4] To help enhance the security of air cargo, the Implementing Recommendations of the 9/11 Commission Act of 2007 (9/11 Commission Act) mandated the Department of Homeland Security (DHS) to establish a system to screen 100 percent of cargo on passenger aircraft—including the domestic and inbound flights of foreign and U.S. passenger operations—by August 2010.[5] The 9/11 Commission Act defines screening for purposes of the air cargo screening mandate as a physical examination or nonintrusive methods of assessing whether cargo poses a threat to transportation security.[6] The act further requires that such a system provide a level of security commensurate with the level of security for the screening of checked baggage. According to TSA, the mission of its air cargo security program is to secure the air cargo transportation system while not unduly impeding the flow of commerce. Although the mandate is applicable to both domestic and inbound cargo, TSA stated that it must address the mandate for domestic and inbound cargo through separate systems because of limitations in its authority to regulate international air cargo industry stakeholders operating outside the United States.

My statement today addresses TSA's progress and challenges in meeting the 9/11 Commission Act mandate to screen air cargo on passenger flights, both domestic cargo and cargo transported from a foreign location to the United States, known as inbound air cargo. My comments are based primarily on our prior reports and testimonies issued from April 2007 through December 2010 addressing the security of the air cargo transportation system, with selected updates in February and March 2011.[7] For these reports, we reviewed documents such as TSA's air cargo security policies and procedures and

Aviation Security 141

conducted site visits to four category X airports and one category I airport in the United States that process domestic and inbound air cargo.[8] We selected these airports based on airport size, passenger and air cargo volumes, location, and participation in TSA's screening program. For the updates, we obtained information on TSA's air cargo security programs and interviewed senior TSA officials regarding plans, strategies, and steps taken to meet the 100 percent screening mandate since December 2010. More detailed information about our scope and methodology is included in our reports and testimonies. We conducted this work in accordance with generally accepted government auditing standards. We shared the information in this statement with TSA officials who provided technical comments that were incorporated as appropriate.

TSA Reports that it Met the Screening Mandate as it Applies to Domestic Cargo, But Previously Identified Data Limitations and other Challenges Persist

TSA took several actions to address the 9/11 Commission Act mandate to screen 100 percent of air cargo as it applies to domestic cargo transported on passenger aircraft by August 2010. As of August 2010, TSA reported that it met the 9/11 Commission Act mandate to screen 100 percent of air cargo as it applies to domestic cargo, although in June 2010 we reported that TSA lacked a mechanism to verify the accuracy of the data used to make this determination.

To help meet the mandate, TSA took several actions, among them:

TSA created a voluntary program to facilitate screening throughout the air cargo supply chain. Since TSA concluded that relying solely on air carriers to conduct screening would result in significant cargo backlogs and flight delays, TSA created the voluntary Certified Cargo Screening Program (CCSP) to allow screening to take place earlier in the shipping process, prior to delivering the cargo to the air carrier. Under the CCSP, facilities at various points in the air cargo supply chain, such as shippers, manufacturers, warehousing entities, distributors, third-party logistics companies, and freight forwarders that are located in the United States, may voluntarily apply to TSA to become certified cargo screening facilities (CCSF).[9] TSA initiated the CCSP at 18 U.S. airports that process high volumes of air cargo, and then expanded the program to all U.S. airports in early 2009.

TSA is taking steps to test technologies for screening air cargo. To test select screening technologies among CCSFs, TSA created the Air Cargo Screening Technology Pilot in January 2008, and selected some of the nation's largest freight forwarders to use these technologies and report on their experiences.[10] In a separate effort, in July 2009, DHS's Directorate for Science and Technology completed the Air Cargo Explosives Detection Pilot Program that tested the performance of select baggage screening technologies for use in screening air cargo at three U.S. airports. In March 2009, TSA initiated a qualification process to test these and other technologies for air carriers and CCSP participants to use in meeting the screening mandate against TSA technical requirements. In December 2009, TSA issued to air carriers and CCSFs its first list of qualified technologies which included X-ray and explosives detection systems (EDS) models that the agency approved for screening air cargo under the 9/11 Commission Act. Over the past several years, TSA has evaluated and qualified additional technologies and has issued subsequent lists, most recently in February 2011. These technologies were in addition to the canine and physical search screening methods permitted by TSA.

TSA expanded its explosives detection canine program. As of February 2011, TSA officials stated that the agency had 113 dedicated air cargo screening canine teams—operating in 20 airports—and was in the process of adding 7 additional canine teams. TSA headquarters officials explained that two CCSFs are participating in a pilot program to test the feasibility of using private canine teams—that meet TSA standards—to inspect air cargo. Officials stated that the pilot is expected to continue through summer 2011.

Even with these actions, TSA continues to face challenges that, among other things, could limit the agency's ability to provide reasonable assurance that screening is being conducted at reported levels. Among the challenges and recommendations previously identified in our June 2010 report are the following.

- *Reported screening data.* TSA does not have a mechanism to verify screening data—which are self-reported by industry representatives. In our June 2010 report, we recommended that TSA develop a mechanism to verify the accuracy of all screening data through random checks or other practical means.[11] TSA partially concurred with our recommendation, and stated that verifying the accuracy of domestic screening data will continue to be a challenge because there is no means to cross-reference local screening logs—which include screening information on specific shipments—with screening reports submitted by air carriers to TSA that do not contain such information. Given that the agency uses these data to report to Congress its compliance with the screening mandate as it applies to domesticcargo, we continue to believe that verifying the accuracy of the screening data is important so that TSA will be better positioned to provide reasonable assurance that screening is being conducted at reported levels.

- Screening technology. TSA has not approved or qualified any equipment to screen cargo transported on unit-load device (ULD) pallets or containers—both of which are common means of transporting air cargo on wide-body passenger aircraft—both domestic and inbound aircraft.[12] Cargo transported on wide-body passenger aircraft makes up 76 percent of domestic air cargo shipments transported on passenger aircraft. The maximum size cargo configuration that may be screened is a 48-by-48-by-65-inch skid— much smaller than the large pallets that are typically transported on wide-body passenger aircraft. Prior to May 1, 2010, canine screening was the only screening method, other than physical search, approved by TSA to screen such cargo configurations. However, effective May 1, 2010, the agency no longer allows canine teams to screen ULD pallets and containers given TSA concerns about the effectiveness of this screening method for those cargo configurations. In addition, TSA is working to complete qualification testing of additional air cargo screening technologies; thus, until all stages of qualification testing are concluded, the agency may not have reasonable assurance that the technologies that air carriers and program participants are currently allowed to use to screen air cargo are effective. TSA is conducting qualification testing to determine which screening technologies are effective at the same time that air carriers are using these technologies to meet the mandated requirement to screen air cargo transported on passenger aircraft. While we recognize that certain circumstances, such as mandated deadlines, require expedited deployment of technologies, our prior work has shown that programs with immature technologies have experienced significant cost and schedule growth.[13]
- Inspection resources. As we reported in June 2010, for domestic air cargo, TSA amended its inspections plan to include inspections of CCSP participants, but the agency had not completed its staffing study

to determine how many inspectors will be necessary to provide oversight of the additional program participants that would support the screening mandate. In our June 2010 report, we recommended that TSA create milestones to help ensure completion of the staffing study. TSA concurred and stated that as part of the staffing study, the agency is working to develop a model to identify the number of required transportation security inspectors and that this effort would be completed in the fall of 2010. As of February 2011, TSA officials stated that the study was in the final stages of review.

TSA Has Taken Steps to Enhance the Security of Inbound Air Cargo, but Previously Identified Screening Data Limitations and other Challenges Persist

TSA has taken a number of steps to enhance the security of inbound air cargo, as discussed below.

TSA moved its deadline for meeting the 100 percent screening mandate as it applies to inbound air cargo. TSA officials stated that they plan to meet the 9/11 Commission Act mandate as it applies to inbound air cargo transported on passenger aircraft by December 2011—2 years earlier than the TSA administrator reported to Congress in November 2010. According to TSA officials, the agency determined it was feasible to require air carriers to meet a December 2011 screening deadline as a result of trends in carrier reported screening data and discussions with air cargo industry leaders regarding progress made by industry to secure inbound cargo on passenger aircraft.

Effective May 1, 2010, air carriers were required to submit inbound screening data to TSA. According to TSA officials, in analyzing this self-reported screening data, TSA found that carriers were screening a higher percentage of air cargo than TSA had initially estimated. For example, TSA previously estimated that 65 percent of inbound cargo by weight would be screened by August 2010. Based on data submitted to TSA by the air carriers, TSA officials stated that the agency estimates that about 80 percent of inbound cargo by weight was screened for the same time period. In addition to requiring air carriers to submit screening data to TSA, in May 2010, TSA also required air carriers to screen a certain percentage of shrink-wrapped and banded inbound cargo.[14] TSA officials stated that in implementing this requirement, air carriers determined that it was more efficient to screen larger groupings of cargo at the point of origin, which resulted in more than the required percentage being screened. Therefore, according to TSA officials, continued progress made by industry will help TSA to meet its December 31, 2011, deadline to screen 100 percent of inbound passenger cargo.

TSA is working with foreign governments to draft international air cargo security standards and to harmonize standards with foreign partners.[15] According to TSA officials, the agency has worked with foreign counterparts over the last 3 years to draft Amendment 12 to the International Civil Aviation Organization's (ICAO) Annex 17, and to generate support for its adoption by ICAO members. The amendment, which was adopted by the ICAO Council in November 2010, will set forth new standards related to air cargo such as requiring members to establish a system to secure the air cargo supply chain (the flow of goods from manufacturers to retailers). TSA has also supported the International Air Transport Association's (IATA) efforts to establish a secure supply chain approach to screening cargo for its member airlines and to have these standards recognized internationally. Moreover, following the October 2010 bomb attempt in cargo originating in Yemen, DHS and TSA, among other things, reached out to international partners, IATA, and the international shipping industry to emphasize the global nature of transportation security threats and the need to strengthen air cargo security through enhanced screening and preventative measures. TSA also deployed a team of security inspectors to Yemen to provide that country's government with assistance and guidance on their air cargo screening procedures.

In November 2010, TSA officials stated that the agency is coordinating with foreign countries to evaluate the comparability of their air cargo security requirements with those of the United States. According to TSA officials, the agency has developed a program, the National Cargo Security Program (NCSP), that would recognize the air cargo security programs of foreign countries if TSA deems those programs provide a level of security commensurate with TSA's programs. TSA plans to coordinate with the top 20 air cargo volume countries, which, according to TSA officials, export about 90 percent of the air cargo transported to the United States on passenger aircraft. According to officials, TSA has completed a review of one country's air cargo security program and has determined that its requirements are commensurate with those of the United States. TSA considers air carriers adhering to NCSP approved programs as being in compliance with TSA air cargo security requirements, according to TSA officials. As of February 2011, TSA continues to evaluate the comparability of air cargo security programs for several other countries. TSA officials stated that although the December 31, 2011, deadline to achieve 100 percent screening is independent of this effort, the agency plans to recognize as many commensurate programs as possible by the deadline.

TSA implemented additional security measures following the October 2010 Yemen air cargo bomb attempt. On November 8, 2010, DHS announced security measures in response to the Yemen incident. TSA banned cargo originating from Yemen and Somalia from transport into the United States; banned the transport of cargo deemed high risk on passenger aircraft; prohibited the transport of toner and ink cartridges weighing 16 ounces or more on passenger aircraft in carry-on and checked luggage; and required additional screening of high-risk cargo prior to transport on an all-cargo aircraft. In addition, TSA is working closely with CBP, industry and international partners to expedite the receipt of advanced cargo data for international flights to the United States prior to departure in order to more effectively identify and screen items based on risk and current intelligence. Further, in December 2010, TSA, CBP, and the air cargo industry launched a new joint technology pilot project referred to as the air cargo advance screening program to enhance the sharing of electronic shipping information to improve the identification of high-risk cargo. In February 2011, TSA officials stated that this effort is currently focused on all-cargo carriers and will expand to passenger carriers in the future.

Even with these steps to improve the security of inbound air cargo, as we previously reported in June 2010, TSA faces challenges that could hinder its ability to meet the 9/11 Commission Act screening mandate as it applies to inbound cargo.

TSA lacks a mechanism to verify data on screening conducted on inbound air cargo. As we reported in June 2010, questions exist about the reliability of TSA's reported screening data for inbound cargo because TSA does not have a mechanism to verify the accuracy of the data reported by industry. In June 2010, we reported that TSA's screening percentages were estimated based on screening requirements of certain countries and were not based on actual data collected from air carriers or other entities, such as foreign governments. In this report, we recommended that TSA develop a mechanism to verify the accuracy of all screening data through random checks or other practical means and obtain actual data on all inbound screening. TSA concurred in part with our recommendation and issued changes to air carriers' standard security programs that required air carriers to report inbound cargo screening data to TSA. However, these requirements apply to air carriers and the screening that they conduct or that may be conducted by a foreign government, but does not reflect screening conducted by other entities throughout the air cargo supply chain. As of March 2011, TSA officials stated that current screening percentages are based on actual data reported by air carriers, but stated that it is difficult to verify the accuracy of the screening data reported by air carriers. Given that TSA now plans to meet the 9/11 Commission Act screening mandate as it applies to inbound air cargo by December 2011, it will be important for TSA to have complete and accurate data in hand to verify that this mandate is being met.

TSA has limited authority to regulate foreign governments or entities. TSA may require that foreign air carriers with operations to, from, or within the United States comply with any applicable requirements, including TSA-issued emergency amendments to air carrier security programs, but foreign countries, as sovereign nations, generally cannot be compelled to implement specific aviation security standards or mutually accept other countries' security measures. International representatives have noted that national sovereignty concerns limit the influence the United States and its foreign partners can have in persuading any country to participate in international harmonization efforts, or make specific changes in their screening procedures. Thus, TSA authority abroad is generally limited to regulating air carrier operations, including the transport of cargo, into the United States. It has no other authority to require foreign governments or entities to, for example, screen a certain percentage of air cargo or screen cargo using specific procedures.

No technology is currently approved or qualified by TSA to screen cargo once it is loaded onto a unit-load device. As we noted earlier for domestic air cargo, TSA has not approved any equipment to screen cargo transported on unit-load device (ULD) pallets or containers—both of which are common means of transporting air cargo on wide-body passenger aircraft—on both domestic and inbound aircraft. As a result, questions remain about air carriers' ability to effectively and efficiently screen air cargo bound for the United States. This is particularly important because, as we reported in June 2010, about 96 percent of inbound air cargo arrives on wide-body aircraft, and TSA has limited authority to oversee the screening activities of foreign governments or entities. We will be examining these issues as part of our ongoing review of TSA's efforts to secure inbound air cargo for the House Committee on Homeland Security and Senate Committee on Homeland Security and Governmental Affairs. We plan to issue the final results later this year.

Mr. Chairman, this concludes my statement. I look forward to answering any questions that you or other members of the subcommittee may have. Individuals making key contributions to this testimony are Steve D. Morris,

Assistant Director; Joel Aldape; Carissa Bryant; Labony Chakraborty; Tom Lombardi; Linda S. Miller; Rebecca Kuhlman Taylor; and Meg Ullengren.

End Notes

[1] For the purposes of this statement, domestic cargo refers to cargo transported by air within the United States and from the United States to a foreign location by both U.S. and foreign air carriers, and inbound cargo refers to cargo transported by both U.S. and foreign air carriers from a foreign location to the United States. These cargo statistics were provided by the Transportation Security Administration from the Bureau of Transportation Statistics.

[2] See Pub. L. No. 107-71, 115 Stat. 597 (2001).

[3] See Pub. L. No. 107-71, § 110(b), 115 Stat. at 614-15 (codified as amended at 49 U.S.C. § 44901).

[4] See 49 U.S.C. § 44901(f) (requiring the system to be in operation as soon as practicable after the date of enactment—November 19, 2001—but without establishing a firm deadline).

[5] See Pub. L. No. 110-53, § 1602(a), 121 Stat. 266, 477-79 (2007) (codified at 49 U.S.C. § 44901(g)).

[6] Although TSA is authorized to approve additional methods for screening air cargo beyond the physical examination or nonintrusive methods listed in the statute, the statute expressly prohibits the use of methods that rely solely on performing a review of information about the contents of cargo or verifying the identity of a shipper. See 49 U.S.C. § 44901(g)(5).

[7] See GAO, *Aviation Security: DHS Has Taken Steps to Enhance International Aviation Security and Facilitate Compliance with International Standards, but Challenges Remain*, GAO-11-238T (Washington, D.C.: Dec. 2, 2010); *Aviation Security: Progress Made but Actions Needed to Address Challenges in Meeting the Air Cargo Screening Mandate*, GAO-10-880T (Washington, D.C.: June 30, 2010); *Aviation Security: TSA Has Made Progress but Faces Challenges in Meeting the Statutory Mandate for Screening Air Cargo on Passenger Aircraft*, GAO-10-446 (Washington, D.C.: June 28, 2010); *Homeland Security: Better Use of Terrorist Watchlist Information and Improvements in Deployment of Passenger Screening Checkpoint Technologies Could Further Strengthen Security*, GAO-10-401T (Washington, D.C.: Jan. 27, 2010); *Aviation Security: Foreign Airport Assessments and Air Carrier Inspections Help Enhance Security, but Oversight of These Efforts Can Be Strengthened*, GAO-07-729 (Washington, D.C.: May 11, 2007); and *Aviation Security: Federal Efforts to Secure U.S.-Bound Air Cargo Are in the Early Stages and Could Be Strengthened*, GAO-07-660 (Washington, D.C.: Apr. 30, 2007).

[8] There are 462 TSA-regulated airports in the United States. TSA classifies the airports it regulates into one of five categories (X, I, II, III, and IV) based on various factors, such as the total number of takeoffs and landings annually, the extent to which passengers are screened at the airport, and other special security considerations. In general, category X airports have the largest number of passenger boardings, and category IV airports have the smallest.

[9] A freight forwarder is a company that consolidates cargo from multiple shippers onto a master air waybill—a manifest of the consolidated shipment—and delivers the shipment to air carriers for transport. For the purpose of this statement, the term freight forwarder only includes those freight forwarders that are regulated by TSA, also referred to as indirect air carriers.

[10] Initially, the Air Cargo Screening Technology Pilot was limited to high-volume freight forwarders (i.e., freight forwarders processing at least 200 shipments annually per location that contain cargo consolidated from multiple shippers). However, in November 2008, TSA issued a second announcement seeking additional high-volume freight forwarders and independent cargo screening facilities to apply for the pilot

[11] http://www.gao.gov/products/GAO-10-880T.

[12] Qualified technologies have undergone a TSA-sponsored test process. Approved technologies are conditionally approved for screening operations for a period of 36 months from the date added to the approved technology list while continuing to undergo further testing for qualification.

[13] See GAO, *Defense Acquisitions: Measuring the Value of DOD's Weapons Programs Requires Starting with Realistic Baselines*, GAO-09-543T (Washington, D.C.: Apr. 1, 2009).

[14] Details on TSA's screening requirements are Sensitive Security Information and are not discussed in this statement. Banded cargo is cargo with heavy-duty metal, plastic, or nylon bands that secure all sides of the cargo shipment or secure the cargo shipment to a skid

[15] Harmonization, as defined by DHS, refers to countries' efforts to coordinate their security standards and practices to enhance security as well as the mutual recognition and acceptance of existing security standards and practices aimed at achieving the same security outcome.

In: Air Cargo Security
Editor: Pierre Turrión

ISBN: 978-1-62100-054-9
© 2012 Nova Science Publishers, Inc.

Chapter 5

STATEMENT OF JOHN SAMMON ASSISTANT ADMINISTRATOR FOR TRANSPORTATION SECTOR NETWORK MANAGEMENT TRANSPORTATION SECURITY ADMINISTRATION U.S. DEPARTMENT OF HOMELAND SECURITY BEFORE THE UNITED STATES HOUSE OF REPRESENTATIVES COMMITTEE ON HOMELAND SECURITY SUBCOMMITTEE ON TRANSPORTATION SECURITY[*]

March 9, 2011

Good afternoon Chairman Rogers, Ranking Member Jackson Lee, and distinguished Members of the Subcommittee. I appreciate the opportunity to appear before you today to discuss the progress that the Transportation Security Administration (TSA) is making in fulfilling air cargo security requirements established by Congress. I thank the Subcommittee for its

---

[*] This is an edited, reformatted and augmented version of Statement given by John Sammon, Assistant Administrator for Transportation Sector Network Management, before the United States House of Representatives Committee on Homeland Security Subcommittee on Transportation Security, dated March 9, 2011.

leadership role in promoting transportation security for the American public, and I look forward to our dialogue today and your thoughts about how we can further improve air cargo security.

TSA is pleased to report that, in conjunction with the air cargo industry, we met the August 2010 mandate included in the Implementing Recommendations of the 9/11 Commission Act of 2007 (9/11 Act) to screen 100 percent of cargo transported on flights of passenger aircraft originating within the United States. A different set of challenges confronts TSA as we continue to make substantial progress toward achieving the 100 percent screening mandate on all international inbound passenger flights to the United States. Additionally, the discovery of explosive devices last October on board aircraft originating in Yemen and ultimately bound for the United States further demonstrated the need for continued vigilance in detecting terrorist devices on board all-cargo aircraft as well as on board passenger aircraft.

Going forward, we need to utilize all available means at our disposal for countering the terrorist threat, developing initiatives with other Department of Homeland Security (DHS) components and offices, and continuing to work collaboratively with our partners internationally and in the private sector. As we pursue intelligence-driven initiatives both domestically and internationally, we will continue to work closely with the Subcommittee in examining how best to protect the traveling public, facilitate the flow of commerce, and guard against the actions of terrorists.

DOMESTIC CARGO SCREENING INITIATIVES MEET STATUTORY REQUIREMENTS

In fulfilling a key provision of the 9/11 Act, last August TSA worked with partners in the air cargo industry to successfully meet the 100 percent cargo screening mandate on domestic and international outbound passenger aircraft on schedule.

We met the deadline within a three-year period with the assistance from a wide spectrum of parties, including air carriers, the shipping industry, freight forwarders and major associations, such as the Air Forwarders Association and the Air Transport Association.

The Certified Cargo Screening Program (CCSP), which was permanently established in 2009 through an Interim Final Rule, has been at the center of industry's overall success. Under this program, responsibility for cargo screening is voluntarily distributed throughout the supply chain to improve security and minimize the bottleneck and potential negative impact on the integrity and movement of commerce that would be created by screening 100 percent of air cargo at the nation's airports. Currently, we have 1,167 entities serving as Certified Cargo Screening Facilities (CCSF), contributing over 54 percent of the total screening volume. Without their participation, the 100 percent screening mandate could not have been met.

TSA must remain vigilant, however, in ensuring that certified companies properly screen air cargo. In FY 2010, TSA increased its cargo inspection force from 450 to 500 and conducted 6,042 inspections on CCSF and airline screening operations. Our training must be comprehensive and compliance must be rigorously enforced. To assist in this effort, TSA recently created and released detailed screening training materials to industry partners. The materials ensure a consistent, high level of training industry-wide on TSA's requirements for cargo handling and screening, facilitate compliance with our security programs, and ultimately drive better security for air cargo.

Participation in the CCSP program is voluntary, but once accepted into the program, a CCSF becomes a regulated party. TSA has a vigorous inspection and compliance program to ensure that CCSP participants are screening as required. If inspections uncover entities violating the spirit and letter of the program requirements, there are a wide range of enforcement actions ranging from voluntary withdrawal from the program to civil enforcement, and if necessary we will undertake criminal enforcement. TSA takes the CCSP program very seriously and we vigorously ensure its integrity.

INTERNATIONAL CARGO SCREENING FACES UNIQUE CHALLENGES

All high-risk cargo on international flights bound for the United States is prohibited from being transported on passenger aircraft. All high risk cargo goes through enhanced security procedures before being shipped on all-cargo aircraft. Nevertheless, complex challenges exist in reaching 100 percent screening of cargo loaded on passenger aircraft inbound to the United States. TSA is working assiduously to meet the international requirement of the 9/11 Act mandate, and recent global events have only further demonstrated the compelling need to heighten security as soon as is practicable. In light of the latest threats and the considerable progress made by air carriers in screening international inbound cargo, TSA has requested industry comment on the feasibility of a proposed deadline of December 31, 2011 to screen 100 percent of the cargo that is transported on passenger aircraft bound for the United States — two years earlier than previously anticipated.

Air carriers were given a 30- to 45-day period (30 days for domestic, 45 days for international carriers) in which to comment on the proposed deadline, after which time TSA will review and evaluate the industry comments prior to making a final determination.

Since passenger air carriers began providing detailed reports on inbound screening percentages in June 2010, it is apparent that more cargo is being screened than TSA had earlier estimated. Many air carriers, including a high number of wide-body operators, are already at or close to 100 percent screening of air cargo inbound to the United States. However, we recognize that closing the final gap poses some operational challenges for airlines. More importantly, TSA does not have the same inspection and compliance authorities overseas that it has in the United States. While TSA can inspect and aggressively pursue enforcement action in the U.S. under the Interim Final Rule, any inspection of air cargo screening overseas requires the full voluntary cooperation of our foreign partners.

To address these challenges, TSA will continue to review other countries' National Country Security Programs (NCSP) to determine whether their programs provide a level of security commensurate with the level of security provided by existing U.S. air cargo security programs. TSA's recognition of other countries' NCSPs will provide us with government oversight of the supply chain and screening process. We are aware that many country programs support a supply chain approach similar to our CCSP. Since we cannot establish a CCSP program overseas, the NCSP approach is a key element in helping industry to accomplish the 100 percent screening goal while also enabling TSA to ensure that inspections and compliance actions are well established by the host government programs and commensurate with U.S. security standards. We are renewing our efforts to ensure broader international awareness of TSA's Congressional screening mandate, and to encourage countries to share their NCSPs with us for review.

In addition, air carriers will be able to use Authorized Representatives to perform screening on their behalf. Authorized Representatives will allow for cargo to be screened by entities such as freight forwarders, operating under the airline program, enabling them to screen the cargo at various points in the supply chain.

SECURITY ARRANGEMENTS FOLLOWING THE AIR CARGO PACKAGES INCIDENT FROM YEMEN

Last October, the global counterterrorism community disrupted a potential attack when individuals in Yemen with ties to al Qaida in the Arabian Peninsula attempted to conceal and ship explosive devices in cargo on board aircraft that traveled through several foreign nations, and ultimately were bound for the United States.

TSA joined with another DHS agency, U.S. Customs and Border Protection (CBP), and immediately initiated additional measures to enhance existing protocols for screening inbound cargo. These included temporarily disallowing all air cargo shipments originating in Yemen destined for the United States and expanding the same policy to include shipments originating in Somalia. TSA has also taken appropriate measures to enhance security requirements for inbound air cargo shipments on passenger and all-cargo planes, and, together with CBP, is in close collaboration with the international shipping community to provide additional security measures for inbound shipments on all-cargo aircraft.

DHS has been working closely with air carriers to continue to refine our counterterrorism strategy based upon focused, measured intelligence-driven protocols. Our measures are designed to produce the maximum security capability without disrupting critical shipping supply chains.

TECHNOLOGY AND EXPLOSIVES DETECTION CANINE TEAMS

TSA's ongoing layered efforts to ensure the highest possible level of security for both domestic and international air cargo include a variety of innovative and cost-effective programs, including an ongoing analysis of technology and the inclusion of authorized representatives to screen on an airline's behalf. We will continue to partner with our international partners and will remain an intelligence-driven agency focused upon detecting, deterring and dismantling attempted terrorist attacks.

Technology will continue to play an important role in screening air cargo. We will continue to evaluate screening technologies to ensure that industry has the most effective equipment at its disposal. Currently, approximately 80 equipment models are fully certified for cargo, up from 20 in February 2009,

In 2010, TSA added a new category of technology, Electro Magnetic Detection (EMD), which has proven to be an effective means of screening products such as perishable commodities.

Our explosives detection canine teams are one of our most reliable resources for cargo screening. These highly effective, mobile teams can quickly locate and identify dangerous materials that may present a threat to cargo and aircraft. Our Proprietary Explosives Detection Canine Teams pair TSA Cargo Inspectors and explosive detection canines to search cargo bound for passenger aircraft. These teams have been deployed to several of our nation's largest airports. They can also be deployed anywhere in the transportation system in support of TSA's mission during periods of heightened security.

Currently, TSA's proprietary canines in the United States perform both primary and secondary (backup) screening at airline facilities in 20 major air cargo gateway cities, screening more than 53 million pounds per month as of January 2011. TSA, working closely with the private sector, has also launched a private sector canine pilot program which, if successful, would enable industry to utilize privately operated teams that meet the same strict standards to which TSA teams are trained and maintained.

CONCLUSION

Thank you for the opportunity to appear before the subcommittee today to discuss TSA's ongoing efforts to increase air cargo security. I look forward to your questions.

INDEX

#

9/11, viii, 2, 5, 11, 17, 20, 21, 22, 28, 34, 42, 43, 50, 52, 53, 58, 64, 66, 67, 69, 74, 75, 77, 78, 79, 81, 84, 85, 87, 89, 90, 91, 96, 109, 110, 113, 115, 118, 120, 121, 124, 137, 140, 141, 142, 144, 146, 147, 152, 153

9/11 Commission, viii, 2, 5, 11, 17, 22, 34, 42, 43, 50, 52, 53, 67, 69, 75, 77, 79, 81, 84, 85, 87, 89, 90, 91, 96, 109, 110, 113, 115, 118, 120, 121, 124, 137, 140, 141, 142, 144, 146, 147, 152

9/11 Commission Act of 2007, viii, 2, 5, 69, 81, 84, 137, 140, 152

A

access, vii, 1, 7, 9, 10, 11, 14, 15, 16, 21, 30, 32, 33, 35, 45, 66, 68, 72, 73, 89, 92
adaptations, 69
agencies, 59, 69, 112, 130, 134
air cargo operations, vii, 1, 2, 6, 7, 8, 9, 11, 13, 23, 30, 33, 35, 36, 38, 39, 46, 48, 49, 56
air cargo system, vii, viii, 1, 2, 5, 17, 39, 58, 81, 99, 137, 139
air carriers, 2, 6, 12, 16, 17, 18, 19, 20, 27, 28, 30, 31, 42, 47, 57, 62, 63, 64, 67, 68, 75, 76, 83, 85, 87, 88, 89, 91, 92, 94, 95, 96, 98, 100, 102, 103, 107, 108, 109, 111, 114, 116, 117, 118, 119, 121, 123, 125, 129, 130, 132, 134, 135, 139, 141, 142, 143, 144,145, 146, 147, 148, 152, 153, 154, 155
airline industry, 44, 52, 75, 78
airports, viii, 5, 6, 15, 23, 27, 28, 31, 32, 33, 37, 45, 49, 57, 61, 65, 66, 69, 76, 81, 85, 87, 89, 92, 96, 98, 99, 100, 102, 105, 107, 109, 114, 129, 131, 141, 142, 148, 153, 156
anthrax, 29
appropriations, 2, 6, 17, 21, 24, 31, 34, 35, 46, 48, 61, 66, 73, 74
Appropriations Act, 6, 15, 21, 22, 30, 66, 89, 119, 132
Arabian Peninsula, 59, 155
asbestos, 50
Asia, 48, 57
assessment, 17, 23, 43, 44, 64, 65, 85, 95, 111, 117, 131
assessment procedures, 85
audit, 20, 30, 68, 76, 87, 141
Austria, 79
authorities, 42, 59, 61, 154
authority, 45, 61, 85, 118, 140, 147
automobile parts, 87
awareness, 31, 72, 104, 154

Index

B

background information, 45
baggage, 5, 6, 7, 10, 11, 13, 14, 21, 22, 24, 25, 26, 33, 38, 39, 40, 42, 43, 46, 49, 58, 59, 60, 61, 66, 67, 69, 70, 84, 85, 96, 97, 108, 131, 140, 142
barriers, 41, 73
base, 48
beams, 35, 37, 40
benefits, 44, 56, 68, 75, 104
border crossing, 37, 70
breakdown, 101, 132
burn, 43, 44
business model, 103
businesses, 5, 76, 134

C

candidates, 98
cargo inspections, vii, 1, 5, 6, 18, 21, 26
cargo workers, vii, 1, 2, 11, 13, 20, 31, 72
Caribbean, 65
cash, 66
catastrophes, 16
category a, 8, 16, 50
certification, 6, 21, 66, 69, 92, 95, 114, 131, 132, 133
Chad, 77
challenges, viii, 5, 17, 27, 29, 30, 38, 46, 61, 62, 67, 68, 70, 81, 82, 83, 85, 87, 90, 97, 99, 102, 104, 107, 108, 110, 113, 115, 117, 118, 120, 121, 122, 124, 138, 139, 140, 142, 146, 152, 153, 154
Chamber of Commerce, 51, 78
chemical, 24, 35, 37, 39, 40, 70, 95, 131
cities, 156
citizens, 29
clothing, 41, 87
CNS, 51, 78
collaboration, 125, 134, 155
commerce, 5, 56, 82, 85, 91, 98, 100, 102, 108, 114, 115, 121, 125, 140, 152, 153

commercial, 10, 21, 41, 56, 77, 85, 108, 129, 130
commodity, 98
community, 86, 155
competitive grant program, 35
complexity, 5, 76
compliance, 19, 21, 26, 30, 31, 32, 56, 60, 61, 62, 63, 69, 76, 86, 89, 92, 94, 105, 106, 111, 113, 124, 133, 135, 143, 145, 153, 154
composition, 39
computed tomography, 35, 38
computer, 5, 38, 131
Conference Report, 89
configuration, 143
Congress, 2, 10, 17, 19, 20, 22, 24, 30, 31, 32, 33, 34, 47, 48, 49, 52, 55, 56, 60, 61, 62, 63, 64, 65, 66, 67, 72, 73, 74, 75, 76, 97, 98, 110, 111, 118, 120, 121, 124, 143, 144, 151
Congressional Budget Office, 20, 26, 52, 53, 61, 77
congressional hearings, 19, 63
consensus, 109
consent, 18, 21
Consolidated Appropriations Act, 33
consolidation, vii, 1, 68, 73, 93
consumers, 27, 67
containers, vii, 2, 11, 23, 36, 37, 39, 40, 42, 43, 44, 56, 57, 68, 69, 70, 71, 73, 75, 82, 91, 100, 101, 102, 103, 107, 114, 121, 125, 133, 143, 147
contingency, 82, 87, 91, 99, 102, 114, 115, 121, 122, 124
control measures, 72, 93
controversial, 74
cooperation, 11, 154
cooperative agreements, 69
coordination, 23, 29, 89, 112, 134
cost, 21, 24, 25, 26, 35, 36, 37, 38, 40, 43, 44, 46, 47, 52, 61, 67, 68, 70, 71, 97, 103, 104, 109, 111, 143, 155
counterfeiting, 20
counterterrorism, 8, 10, 155
counterterrorism strategy, 155

Index

country of origin, 66
covering, 24
credentials, 14, 32
crimes, 13, 14
criminal activities, vii, 1
criminal activity, 13, 36
critical infrastructure, 55
CT scan, 37
customers, 5, 19, 28, 47, 64, 103
Customs and Border Protection, 23, 56, 83, 84, 155

D

data collection, 86, 99, 119
database, 2, 17, 18, 20, 63, 64, 117
deadly force, 33, 74
deficiencies, 76, 95
deficit, 26
Department of Commerce, 86
Department of Homeland Security (DHS), vi, viii, 2, 5, 6, 17, 22, 23, 24, 29, 35, 43, 48, 49, 51, 52, 53, 67, 78, 81, 83, 84, 85, 87, 89, 96, 97, 109, 111, 119, 123, 125, 132, 133, 137, 140, 142, 145, 146, 148, 149, 152, 155
Department of Justice, 13, 14
Department of Transportation (DOT), 12, 19, 49, 50, 51, 76, 77, 78
depth, 76
designers, 45
detection, vii, 2, 5, 6, 7, 12, 14, 21, 22, 23, 24, 25, 28, 35, 36, 37, 38, 39, 40, 43, 47, 49, 64, 67, 69, 70, 71, 83, 89, 96, 97, 98, 110, 131, 132, 138, 142, 156
detection system, 7, 21, 22, 23, 28, 37, 39, 40, 67, 69, 83, 89, 142
detonation, 11, 45
direct costs, 26, 27, 44
directives, 89, 118
distribution, 2, 5, 8, 13, 47, 56, 76
District of Columbia, 51
diversity, 57, 62
dogs, 24, 69, 135
domestic markets, 57

draft, 62, 123, 145
drugs, 37

E

economic damage, 60
economic downturn, 95
economic growth, 57
education, 111
electronic systems, 36, 71
emergency, 11, 14, 58, 118, 147
employees, 6, 15, 16, 19, 26, 33, 45, 56, 67, 68, 89, 92, 94
employers, 68
energy, 40
enforcement, 12, 30, 61, 69, 130, 153, 154
environment, vii, 2, 5, 38, 40, 49, 69, 96, 97, 99, 103, 104, 109, 110, 130
equipment, 6, 21, 22, 32, 35, 38, 39, 40, 49, 56, 66, 67, 87, 96, 97, 98, 103, 104, 143, 147, 155
Europe, 24, 57
European Commission, 83, 116
European Union, 62
Everglades, 12, 50
evidence, 10, 59, 87
evolution, 5
exercise, 117
expenditures, 46
expertise, 13, 96
explosives, vii, 1, 5, 6, 7, 9, 10, 11, 12, 15, 16, 17, 19, 21, 22, 23, 24, 25, 29, 35, 36, 37, 38, 39, 40, 41, 42, 47, 49, 50, 55, 59, 60, 61, 63, 64, 65, 67, 69, 70, 73, 83, 89, 96, 97, 98, 107, 109, 131, 132, 135, 138, 142, 156
exports, 4
express packages, vii, 1, 2, 21, 38

F

FAA, 12, 19, 20, 40, 42, 43, 44, 52, 57, 63, 73, 77
factories, 68

Index

federal agency, viii, 81, 137
Federal Bureau of Investigation (FBI), 11, 50
federal government, 19, 46, 115
Federal Register, 51, 52, 53, 78
fiber, 36, 71
financial, 67, 70, 103, 104
fire suppression, 44
firearms, 16, 33, 34, 74
fires, 35
fiscal year 2009, 94, 98, 99, 105, 130
fish, 57
flexibility, 94, 102, 103
flights, viii, 3, 10, 11, 14, 15, 16, 24, 32, 33, 34, 35, 42, 43, 45, 46, 56, 57, 58, 59, 60, 61, 62, 63, 65, 67, 69, 73, 74, 75, 81, 84, 91, 92, 112, 113, 118, 131, 134, 139, 140, 141, 146, 152, 153
flowers, 4, 57
force, 14, 153
Fourth Amendment, 28
fruits, 57
fuel consumption, 75
funding, 6, 31, 33, 35, 40, 46, 48, 49, 61, 73, 104, 132
funds, 31, 61

G

Germany, 59, 62, 77
global trade, 4
governments, 13, 89, 116, 119, 121, 123, 139, 145, 146, 147
GPS, 36
graph, 29
Greece, 59, 77
growth, 3, 57, 77, 109, 143
growth rate, 57
guidance, 23, 26, 45, 98, 105, 109, 110, 132, 145
guidelines, 19, 30, 32, 63, 86, 112, 132

H

harmonization, 134, 147
hazardous materials, vii, 1, 9, 12, 14, 16, 19, 63
hazardous substances, 28
hiring, 31, 49, 61, 103
history, 11, 33, 94
homeland security, 41
Homeland Security Act, 33, 34, 74
Homeland Security Subcommittee on Transportation Security, vi, viii, 151
Hong Kong, 70
House of Representatives, v, vi, viii, 52, 84, 151
human, 38, 70, 87, 131
human remains, 87

I

ideal, 100, 101, 109
identification, vii, 2, 15, 29, 31, 32, 33, 35, 36, 71, 146
identity, 45, 90, 148
illegal shipments of hazardous materials, vii, 1
image, 38, 41, 70
imaging systems, 35, 41
immigration, 131
imports, 4, 119
improvements, 48, 103
India, 10, 50
individuals, 7, 9, 11, 14, 15, 16, 21, 28, 30, 32, 33, 34, 62, 66, 76, 88, 134, 155
industries, 46, 95, 102
industry-wide consolidation, vii, 1
information sharing, 134
information technology, 92
injuries, 14, 58
insertion, 24
inspections, vii, 1, 2, 5, 6, 10, 12, 16, 18, 21, 22, 23, 24, 26, 30, 31, 36, 39, 46, 48, 49, 60, 62, 64, 66, 76, 86, 89, 94, 104, 105, 106, 111, 132, 133, 143, 153, 154

Index

inspectors, 2, 30, 49, 61, 62, 76, 82, 87, 89, 104, 105, 106, 107, 111, 121, 133, 144, 145
integration, 14
integrity, 18, 20, 31, 32, 35, 63, 71, 72, 86, 112, 153
intelligence, 59, 131, 146, 152, 155
International Atomic Energy Agency, 79
investment, 39
Ireland, 10, 50
Israel, 73
issues, 13, 14, 20, 30, 83, 87, 109, 139, 147

J

jurisdiction, 118
justification, 7, 132

L

landings, 129, 148
law enforcement, 8, 13, 14, 59, 61, 69, 89, 130
laws, 13, 30, 66, 112
laws and regulations, 30, 112
leadership, 26, 152
legislation, 2, 7, 17, 26, 28, 34, 60, 73
legislative proposals, 47
light, 4, 37, 111, 153
liquids, 50
logistics, 30, 57, 64, 68, 73, 92, 141
luggage, 14, 58, 146

M

machinery, 87
magnitude, 42
majority, 26, 92, 103, 104, 134
management, 14, 85, 87, 106, 112, 120, 124, 130
manufactured goods, 47, 56, 103
manufacturing, 4, 48, 56
marketplace, 5
mass, 10, 132

materials, 12, 28, 37, 39, 40, 41, 43, 50, 70, 94, 153, 156
matter, 96
measurement, 112, 124
media, 10, 59
medical, 87
methodology, 65, 101, 105, 117, 129, 141
Mexico, 65, 134
Miami, 10, 13, 50, 62, 63
migration, 48
mission, 65, 85, 115, 140, 156
models, 5, 96, 142, 155
modifications, 110
Montana, 50

N

National Public Radio, 52
National Research Council, 40, 43, 53
national security, 55, 135
neutrons, 40
nonenforcement, 132, 133
North America, 130
Northwest Airlines, 8
nuclear weapons, 37

O

Office of Management and Budget, 51, 86, 99, 112, 130, 133
Office of the Inspector General, 19, 50, 51, 78
operating revenues, 27, 68
operating system, 45
operations, vii, 1, 2, 6, 7, 8, 9, 11, 13, 14, 23, 28, 30, 31, 32, 33, 35, 36, 38, 39, 43, 46, 47, 48, 49, 56, 58, 62, 74, 84, 85, 105, 140, 147, 149, 153
opportunities, 5
organic peroxides, 50
outreach, 82, 95, 103, 104, 131
oversight, vii, 1, 6, 12, 19, 20, 21, 26, 30, 31, 32, 46, 64, 76, 91, 99, 105, 106, 112, 122, 123, 124, 131, 144, 154

oxygen, 12

P

Pacific, 58, 98
Pakistan, 58
parallel, 64
participants, 34, 68, 74, 82, 89, 92, 94, 95, 96, 97, 102, 103, 104, 106, 108, 121, 142, 143, 153
passenger airline, 5, 8, 9, 23, 25, 27, 28, 31, 33, 34, 41, 55, 59, 67, 72, 73, 74
passenger travel, 119
pattern recognition, 45
penalties, 13, 15
per capita cost, 103
pharmaceuticals, 91, 95, 102
Philippines, 11, 58
pilot study, 107
point of origin, 144
police, 130
policy, vii, 7, 11, 20, 29, 44, 45, 55, 56, 60, 65, 75, 98, 99, 155
policy issues, 56
policy options, vii
policymakers, viii, 5, 44, 55, 66, 73
population, 55, 132
President, 29, 49, 51, 52, 61, 78
President Clinton, 51, 78
principles, 39
private firms, 56
probability, 38, 39
probe, 37, 40
producers, 95
profit, 27, 68
profit margin, 27
profitability, 27, 67
project, 24, 86, 87, 106, 113, 121, 130, 146
protection, 21, 33, 66
public policy, 25
Puerto Rico, 32

Q

quality control, 86
questioning, 28

R

radiation, 40
radio, 36, 71
reactions, 40
recognition, 86, 149, 154
recommendations, 12, 14, 19, 43, 63, 82, 111, 123, 138, 142
redundancy, 16
reengineering, 130
reform, 2, 6, 12, 20, 35, 42, 45, 64, 75
regulations, 2, 6, 7, 15, 16, 17, 20, 21, 30, 31, 34, 60, 61, 62, 73, 91, 92, 115
regulatory changes, 45
regulatory oversight, 30, 76
regulatory requirements, 119
reinforcement, 44
reliability, 86, 91, 111, 146
requirements, 7, 9, 17, 20, 21, 26, 27, 30, 32, 38, 41, 45, 47, 48, 49, 59, 60, 61, 62, 65, 67, 69, 72, 82, 88, 89, 91, 93, 94, 95, 96, 98, 102, 103, 104, 105, 106, 107, 108, 110, 111, 113, 114, 115, 117, 118, 119, 121, 123, 132, 133, 134, 135, 142, 145, 146, 147, 149, 151, 153, 155
resistance, 42, 43
resolution, 70
resources, 22, 27, 31, 46, 64, 67, 82, 90, 95, 103, 105, 106, 121, 122, 123, 125, 143, 156
response, 10, 16, 28, 34, 38, 60, 76, 85, 104, 111, 113, 134, 146
restrictions, 9, 28, 29
revenue, 3, 26, 28, 42, 43, 77
rights, 29
rings, 13
risk, 2, 7, 9, 10, 11, 12, 14, 16, 17, 18, 22, 24, 34, 42, 43, 44, 46, 48, 55, 56, 59, 60, 62, 63, 64, 65, 66, 74, 75, 84, 99, 105,

Index

115, 116, 118, 120, 122, 139, 140, 146, 153
risk assessment, 17, 23, 64, 65
risk profile, 65
risks, vii, 1, 8, 9, 11, 22, 33, 44, 64, 75, 102, 119
routes, 27, 52, 57, 67, 93
rules, 11, 17, 20, 33, 64, 92

S

sabotage, vii, 1, 9, 14, 15, 16
safety, 12, 19, 20, 29, 40, 45, 63
Saudi Arabia, 59
scatter, 37
scope, 76, 141
screening mandate, viii, 23, 61, 62, 68, 69, 81, 82, 83, 84, 85, 87, 90, 91, 95, 96, 99, 100, 101, 102, 103, 105, 106, 107, 108, 114, 115, 116, 117, 118, 119, 120, 121, 122, 124, 125, 126, 129, 132, 138, 139, 140, 141, 142, 143, 144, 146, 147, 152, 153, 154
SEA, 23
security risks, vii, 1, 9
security training, vii, 1, 34, 60, 72, 74
Senate, 20, 48, 51, 60, 61, 64, 84, 132, 147
sensing, 35
sensors, 24
services, 76, 132
shortage, 107
signals, 71
Singapore, 70
smuggling, vii, 1, 9, 13, 52
software, 57
solution, 17, 23, 70
Somalia, 59, 77, 146, 155
South America, 134
sovereignty, 147
specifications, 43, 45
spectroscopy, 40
spending, 26
SSI, 79
staffing, 37, 82, 86, 104, 105, 106, 121, 122, 123, 143

stakeholders, viii, 6, 7, 22, 24, 26, 27, 35, 43, 49, 56, 64, 67, 81, 82, 85, 89, 94, 96, 98, 100, 101, 103, 107, 108, 114, 121, 125, 132, 140
state, 59, 60, 61, 113, 121, 134
state authorities, 134
statistics, 4, 13, 77, 129, 130, 131, 134, 148
statutes, 13
storage, 44
structure, 42
suicide, 8, 10
supervisor, 15
suppliers, 48
supply chain, vii, 1, 14, 18, 23, 24, 26, 36, 39, 49, 56, 62, 64, 68, 70, 71, 72, 82, 90, 92, 95, 99, 102, 104, 108, 114, 116, 118, 120, 125, 134, 138, 141, 145, 147, 153, 154, 155
surveillance, 72

T

target, 7, 10, 11, 55, 59, 105, 116, 118, 120, 133, 139
tariff, 13
technical comments, 126, 138, 141
techniques, 5, 6, 21, 24, 35, 37, 66, 99
technologies, vii, 2, 5, 6, 14, 17, 18, 19, 21, 22, 23, 25, 29, 35, 36, 37, 38, 40, 41, 45, 47, 48, 49, 65, 66, 67, 69, 70, 71, 85, 89, 91, 96, 97, 98, 99, 107, 108, 109, 110, 130, 132, 138, 142, 143, 149, 155
technology, vii, 1, 2, 5, 14, 17, 23, 24, 26, 32, 34, 35, 36, 37, 39, 40, 41, 42, 43, 45, 46, 47, 60, 65, 70, 71, 82, 85, 91, 94, 97, 99, 103, 104, 107, 108, 109, 110, 113, 121, 122, 124, 130, 131, 132, 138, 143, 146, 147, 149, 155, 156
technology-based initiatives, vii, 1
terminals, 14, 66
terrorism, 11, 16, 51, 129
terrorist activities, 13
terrorist organization, 11, 59
terrorist watchlist, 68

terrorists, 7, 10, 11, 15, 19, 34, 44, 58, 60, 63, 84, 89, 99, 129, 140, 152
testing, 6, 35, 40, 41, 49, 86, 89, 91, 96, 97, 98, 99, 107, 108, 109, 110, 132, 143, 149
testing program, 99, 132
theft, vii, 1, 9, 13, 15, 36, 71
thoughts, 152
threats, vii, 1, 2, 10, 11, 14, 31, 41, 55, 58, 65, 70, 97, 109, 110, 119, 145, 153
time factors, 40
time frame, 21, 86, 95, 106, 111, 117, 118, 120, 122
time pressure, 38
total revenue, 27
trade, 56, 61, 95
training, vii, 1, 24, 30, 31, 33, 34, 37, 38, 47, 49, 60, 69, 72, 74, 89, 92, 94, 95, 103, 153
training programs, 60, 92
transactions, 116
transmission, 36, 37, 71
transport, 4, 5, 8, 12, 16, 17, 18, 21, 27, 34, 57, 88, 117, 123, 125, 130, 131, 139, 146, 147, 148
transportation, viii, 3, 7, 13, 14, 24, 45, 51, 58, 62, 76, 83, 84, 89, 102, 110, 111, 115, 122, 138, 140, 144, 145, 152, 156
transportation security, 7, 13, 45, 62, 76, 83, 84, 89, 140, 144, 145, 152
Transportation Security Administration, vi, viii, 2, 51, 52, 53, 55, 77, 78, 79, 81, 83, 84, 129, 134, 137, 139, 148, 151
Treasury, 52
TSA officials, viii, 37, 81, 83, 85, 87, 92, 94, 95, 96, 99, 100, 101, 102, 103, 104, 105, 106, 107, 108, 109, 110, 112, 113, 115, 117, 118, 119, 120, 131, 133, 134, 135, 138, 139, 141, 142, 144, 145, 146, 147

U

U.S. airports, viii, 65, 81, 92, 96, 99, 141, 142

uniform, 134
unit cost, 43
United Airlines, 73
United Kingdom (UK), 10, 50, 53, 59, 77, 119
United Nations, 116, 134
United States (USA), viii, 3, 4, 8, 9, 11, 13, 16, 17, 29, 48, 50, 51, 52, 53, 56, 57, 59, 60, 61, 62, 65, 72, 77, 78, 79, 81, 84, 87, 89, 92, 116, 118, 119, 129, 131, 134, 135, 137, 138, 139, 140, 141, 145, 146, 147, 148, 151, 152, 153, 154, 155, 156

V

validation, 92, 131
vehicles, 21, 30, 32, 66
Vice President, 51, 78
vulnerability, 11, 31, 49, 65, 73, 76, 113, 118, 124, 131

W

Washington, 49, 50, 51, 52, 53, 77, 78, 79, 130, 131, 133, 134, 148, 149
water, 4
weapons, 8, 15, 32, 41, 89
weapons of mass destruction, 8, 58, 89, 131
White House, 19, 51, 52, 63, 78
wires, 97
withdrawal, 153
workers, vii, 1, 2, 11, 13, 15, 20, 31, 32, 33, 68, 72
workforce, 62, 76, 105, 106
working conditions, 38
workload, 106
worldwide, 5, 57, 62

Y

Yemen, 59, 60, 77, 139, 145, 146, 152, 155